IN AND AROUND
SOUTH TYNEDALE AND

Ian Smith

sandhill press

My thanks go to those who have encouraged me, with snippets of information, good company and excellent conversation.

to Mums and Dads.

The section maps are mostly to a scale of about 1:45 000, and are based on Ordnance Survey Landranger Sheets 86 (1984) and 87 (1985), or to a scale of about 1:22 000 based on Ordnance Survey Pathfinder Sheet 546 (1990). The chapter maps are to a scale of about 1:220 000, based on Ordnance Survey Routemaster mapping, with the permission of the Controller of Her Majesty's Stationery Office.
© Crown Copyright 83256M

First published in Great Britain by Sandhill Press Ltd, 17 Castle Street, Warkworth, MORPETH, Northumberland, NE65 0UW, 1997.

© Ian Smith 1997.

Purchasers and readers are asked to note the section on 'Public Rights of Way and Private Property.' No part of this publication is intended or should be construed as encouragement to trespass.

ISBN 0 946908 46 8

Printed and bound by Martins of Berwick.
Cover design by Linda K Graphic Design Studio.

CONTENTS

The South Tyne at Featherstone Bridge.

Lanercost Priory, built with stone from Hadrian's Wall:

INTRODUCTION.

Walking down the South Tyne valley is a walk through history. The start, high on Cross Fell or at Tyne Head, takes you back to a period before man, when the hills were lonely. But signs of mankind soon appear, even on the high fells — and industrial man too. From very early times these hills were worked for their lead, and relics of the mines abound. The precious lead — and silver — brought the Romans here too, and helped ensure that the South Tyne was included within the Roman Empire, south of Hadrian's Wall. Mining gave substance to towns like Garrigill and Alston, Haltwhistle and Bardon Mill, and they still show signs of their mining roots.

But the South Tyne yielded good farmland too. This was the granary of northern England for centuries. The farmers that came with the legions must have recognised the worth of those gentle south-facing slopes, on the north bank of the river. Why else choose to defend the rocky crags to the north rather than make the economic border along the river?

The mines and farms brought prosperity — and envy. Once control of Northumberland moved out of the hands of local kings the area became a political football for the kings of England and Scotland: far enough away for the cries of the inhabitants not to matter too much, a place to hold battles when diplomacy failed or a gesture against an external enemy was needed. Northumberland and the South Tyne valley suffered. It became a land of castles great and small, where every farm and vicarage needed a defensive tower, a land where war ate the prosperity of the land.

After the Union between Scotland and England stability returned and the wealth of land and mines restored prosperity. The mineral wealth is now largely worked out, but the valley has continued an industrial tradition in little pockets. Some travellers may think these out of place in a landscape now largely pastoral, but this is sentimentality: Northumberland has a strong industrial tradition, even in the "countryside" and does not throw it away lightly.

This book offers a walk through this history. Look for it as you go. There are plenty of signs, some obvious, like the Roman Wall and the churches, some for the more alert to find, like mine levels and lime kilns. Some are pointed out in the text, but there is plenty for the observant to find for themselves.

The guide falls naturally into four parts:

1) — beside the young South Tyne in its headlong rush from the high Pennines to the lusher valley, passing through Garrigill and Alston to Haltwhistle.

The infant river below Tyne Head.

2) — continuing alongside a more placid South Tyne as it wends through farmland on its way to Hexham. For variety there are excursions up the wild river Allen, and to Roman Vindolanda, and diversions up onto moorland where roads monopolise the river-banks.

Roman Wall on Cawfield Crags

3) – along the Roman Wall, from Brampton to Chollerford. Although not the entire Wall, this shows much of the best.

4) – the town of Hexham. A town trail and a look at the Abbey complete the tour.

Hexham Abbey.

The guide can be used by serious walkers wanting a long continuous walk, or by day-walkers who want short routes that are circular or have public transport links. The page by page layout tries to offer such return routes, although this is not easy above Garrigill!

Linear walkers can start at Garrigill (taxi from Alston), or Dufton (bus or taxi from Appleby), heading over Cross Fell to Tyne Head, then downriver to Haltwhistle. The riverside route can be followed – with excursions – to Hexham. A bus or train to Brampton allows the Roman Wall to be started, and the guide returns you eventually to Hexham.

Day walkers can dip into the book almost anywhere, and find short linear walks with public transport for returns, or with alternative return routes. Some of the public transport only operates in summer.

Public Transport.

Bus services.

Bus services and operators can change at short notice. Please check current information with operators or in the Northumberland Public Transport Guide.

At present:

Northumbria Motor Services operate a frequent service between Newcastle and Carlisle, that serves Hexham, Haydon Bridge, Bardon Mill, Haltwhistle and Greenhead, Gilsland and Brampton.

Haydon Bridge, Langley and Staward (station) are also served by their Hexham - Allendale service.

Wright Bros (Nenthead) operate services between Alston and Haltwhistle, via Slaggyford and Lambley, that connect with train services at Haltwhistle.

They also operate a Newcastle - Keswick service via Hexham, Haydon Bridge, Langley, Cupola Bridge and Alston.

Tyne Valley coaches operate between Hexham, Acomb and Chollerford with their Colwell and Bellingham buses, and also from Hexham to West Boat, Fourstones and Newbrough.

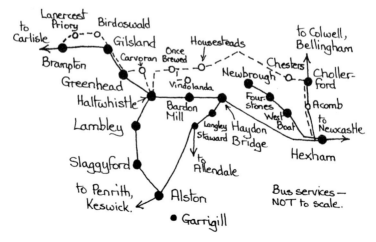

8

Hadrian's Wall Bus Services.

During the summer there are often bus services to and from places on the Wall. From Hexham a service operates to Chollerford, Chesters, Brocolitia, Housesteads, Vindolanda, Once Brewed and Haltwhistle. Another links Haltwhistle, Greenhead, Gilsland, Birdoswald, Lanercost and Brampton.

Trains.

At the time of writing Regional Railways (North-East) operate trains along the Newcastle - Hexham - Carlisle line.

A roughly half-hourly service connects Newcastle and Hexham.

Trains connect Hexham, Haltwhistle and Carlisle roughly hourly during the day.

A few trains call at Bardon Mill, Haydon Bridge and Brampton. The station at Brampton is distant from the town.

Some trains operate to farther afield, to Glasgow, Middlesbrough and Sunderland.

EQUIPMENT FOR WALKERS.

On warm balmy days you can wander around Hexham without any special gear at all. But out on the Roman Wall and up on the hills it is well to be prepared. The Wall can be very bleak indeed, and Cross Fell catches the rain whichever way the wind blows:

' If you can't see the top of Cross Fell its raining;
  if you can see the top of Cross Fell its about to rain,'

<u>Windproof and waterproof</u> gear are essential – even if they stay in the rucksack most of the time.

<u>Boots</u> too are a good idea for the fells and the Wall. You will meet rough crags, rocky staircases, bogs and morasses.

<u>Hats and gloves</u> protect vulnerable heads and hands from cold in winter, and ultraviolet whenever the sun shines, at any time of year. Sun-block is useful too.

<u>Binoculars</u> are useful for route-finding as well as bird-watching, for finding yellow arrows on walls as well as yellowhammers on top branches. A lightweight camera will help you remember the joys of your days out.

<u>Maps.</u> Even with this guide in your pocket it is worthwhile to carry good Ordnance Survey maps. The 1:50 000 Landranger maps will put your route in a wider context, and allow you to identify those hills, chimneys, roads, etc several miles away from the route.
Useful sheets are:

91, "Appleby in Westmoreland" for Cross Fell,
86, " Haltwhistle, Bewcastle and Alston",
87, " Hexham, Haltwhistle and Surroundings"

<u>Compass.</u> If you know how to use it, it will be useful on the Cross Fell section. If you do not know how to use it then stay off Cross Fell!

RIGHTS OF WAY and PRIVATE PROPERTY

Wherever possible, the routes indicated on the section maps use public rights of way or permissive paths, for pedestrians.

Rights of way allow you the normal activities of progression, including stopping to admire the scenery, or to eat lunch. They do not allow you to camp, light fires, leave litter or indulge in antisocial behaviour.
Permissive paths are at the discretion of the land-owner, and may have more restrictive rules. These usually exclude permissive behaviour!

Some parts of the routes suggest visits to private property, where you may be asked for an entrance fee or for a donation towards upkeep. These include National Trust and English Heritage properties along the Wall (eg Chesters, Birdoswald, Housesteads), Vindolanda, Hexham Abbey and the National Trust countryside at Allen Banks & Staward. Nothing in this guide suggests that you have any rights to visit these properties, but you will probably be made very welcome at reasonable times of day.

SECTION MAPS...

are mostly at a scale of about 1:45 000 
All maps are the right way up, ie north at the top!

Symbols include:

– – – – –	suggested route
• • • • • • • •	alternative route (or suggested route in built-up areas).
·········· 100 ·······	contours (50m intervals).
~~	river or stream
═══════	road
▪·▪▪▪ ♠♣♠♣	buildings, trees.
g s ls	gate, stile, ladder-stile (where helpful).
─┬─┬─┬─	some field boundaries are shown to help clarity.
– – ⑨ – –	distance from start of section (in km).

Route directions are in boxes, marked with ✳
Alternative route directions are marked with �֎

Notes on points of interest are indicated with ●

HADRIAN'S WALL — a brief history.

The Romans had been in Britain for about sixty years before they started work on the Wall. They had gone much further north than this, establishing roads and forts in Scotland as far as the River Tay. The Tyne Gap had a strategic value, allowing troops to be moved relatively easily between the high-road through Corbridge and the western road through Carlisle. To help with this movement a road was built between the two — the Stanegate. You will meet this at Vindolanda, and as the road down into Newbrough.

As pressures mounted in Scotland around AD90 the Romans consolidated, drawing back from their most distant outposts and reinforcing the Tyne Gap. A line of forts was built along the Stanegate. You meet these at Carvoran, Haltwhistle Burn and Vindolanda.

After Trajan died in 117AD Hadrian became Emperor, and spent some time securing his position in Rome before touring his empire. From his time on the Eastern Front he knew about border control, and after his visit to Britain orders went out for the Wall to be built. It used the high ground just north of the Stanegate and stretched from Wallsend on the Tyne to Bowness on Solway, walling off northern Britain.

It was built in an organised military way: the 3metre wide foundation first, followed by milecastles and turrets. Then the curtain wall was added in between.

The technology improved as they built. The early wall was the full 3 metres thick, with stone faces infilled with rubble and puddled clay. Some bright engineer realised that the wall could be made thinner, and cheaper, if they used mortar with the rubble infill, without losing strength or stability. So in places you will find narrow Wall built on broad bases, and narrow (2 metre-wide) Wall joining onto the original broad wings of the already-built turrets. Watch out for changes of gauge as you follow excavated sections of Wall.

There are also places where the Wall was not built on the original line of foundations for some reason. Look for this on the high ground just east of milecastle 39.

Another feature of the defences was the Ditch, on the north side of the Wall. This was dug wherever there were no crags immediately in front of the Wall, inhibiting use of rams and frontal assaults.

After nearly two thousand years this Ditch is still a very prominent feature, and is clearly seen alongside the ridge road from Banks to Birdoswald, and again beside Wade's Military Road from Sewingshields to Limestone Corner. It is also the most prominent feature up the hillside east of Thirlwall Castle.

These features combined to give a very effective economic & population control barrier, with access only at the milecastles. It was similar in concept to the Iron Curtain across Europe - and Hadrian did build a wall - a wooden one - across Germany too.

Sometime during construction there was a major change of plan. The forts, which would have been in the rear, down on the Stanegate, were moved up onto the Wall. These new forts included Birdoswald, Great Chesters, Housesteads, Brocolitia and Chesters, that you will meet en route.

HADRIAN'S WALL (continued).

Some of the new forts were sited to protect strategic weak points in the Wall, such as the river crossings at Chesters and Willowford. Others filled in the gaps, or were added in the light of experience. Some housed infantry, and others cavalry. Parts of the Wall, and some turrets and milecastles had to be destroyed in order to place the forts in their best positions.

Another feature added at this time was the <u>Vallum</u>. This deep ditch, with an earth bank on each side, was on the South side of the Wall. Sometimes it was close to it, as at Limestone Corner, sometimes well to the south, as on Haltwhistle Common. It helped define a military zone along the Wall, but cannot have been a great success. Within a very few years it was at least partially filled in, and never re-instated. Perhaps it was more of a nuisance to the army than to the north Britons.

Much of the Wall system was complete by Hadrian's death in 138 AD. It was one of the wonders of the world : a coast-to-coast wall about 5 metres high, stone-built from Wallsend to Willowford, and turf-built from there to the Solway coast. It had milecastles and turrets. It may even have been rendered and whitewashed. What a sight it must have been!

But Antonius Pius, the new Emperor, had other ideas. He sent the legions back into Scotland and built his own Turf Wall from Forth to Clyde. The milecastles on Hadrian's Wall were thrown open to traffic and the turrets abandoned.

Fifteen years of Scotland were too much. In the 150's the Romans began to set Hadrian's Wall back in order, and by 163 AD the Romans had pulled back from the Antonine Wall. On Hadrian's Wall the milecastles were repaired and the forts re-occupied. Some of the turrets were demolished and replaced by plain Wall. (You can see this in the ruins of turrets east of Sewingshields). At some stage the Turf Wall west of the Irthing was replaced by a new Stone Wall, some of it on a new alignment. A new Military Way was added, linking forts and milecastles on the south side of the Wall.

Hadrian's Wall was there to stay. Evidence of building work continues until at least 300 AD. Compare its long active period with the mere forty years of the Iron Curtain.

Around the forts towns sprang up. You can see a little of the town at Housesteads, and plenty at Vindolanda.

But at some stage, as the Empire retracted at the end of the 4th century, even the Wall was abandoned. During the Dark Age — and later — the Wall was understandably robbed of its dressed stone. Lanercost Priory is built of local Wall sandstone — a lovely red colour; while Hexham contains much stone carted from Corbridge. Other Roman stones contribute to the solidly-built, and sometimes very ancient farm-houses along the Wall.

Major demolition occurred during the 17th century. During the Stuart adventures into England the government found difficulty in moving modern armies from Newcastle to Carlisle. General Wade built a new road. For many miles, from Newcastle to Carrawburgh, the Roman Wall provided not only a plentiful source of stone, but an excellent base too. The Wall disappeared, and its footings are still under the modern road. Odd fragments — a stretch of Wall here, a turret there — survive beside the road, and are worth looking for as a post-script to this walk.

Between Birdoswald and Banks the Wall disappeared under a road too, flanked by Ditch and Vallum. West of Banks the Wall was largely re-absorbed into the farmlands of the Eden valley, and in Newcastle it disappeared under housing — with some amazing relics in suburban gardens!

But between Birdoswald and Sewingshields the Wall is largely still there — reduced in height, sometimes yet to be excavated — a testament to the Roman engineers who built it.

Brunton Turret — east of Chollerford.

Chapter One: the High South Tyne.

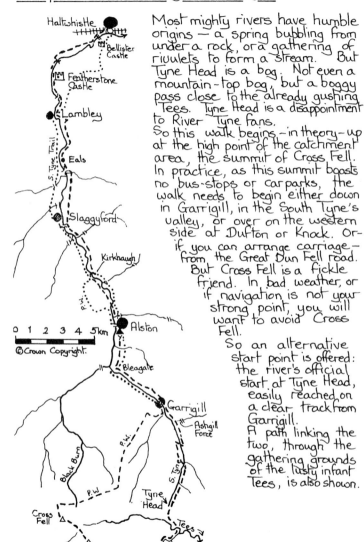

Most mighty rivers have humble origins — a spring bubbling from under a rock, or a gathering of rivulets to form a stream. But Tyne Head is a bog. Not even a mountain-top bog, but a boggy pass close to the already gushing Tees. Tyne Head is a disappointment to River Tyne fans.

So this walk begins — in theory — up at the high point of the catchment area, the summit of Cross Fell. In practice, as this summit boasts no bus-stops or carparks, the walk needs to begin either down in Garrigill, in the South Tyne's valley, or over on the western side at Dufton or Knock. Or — if you can arrange carriage — from the Great Dun Fell road. But Cross Fell is a fickle friend. In bad weather, or if navigation is not your strong point, you will want to avoid Cross Fell.

So an alternative start point is offered: the river's official start at Tyne Head, easily reached on a clear track from Garrigill.

A path linking the two, through the gathering grounds of the lusty infant Tees, is also shown.

Haltwhistle

Bellister Castle

Featherstone Castle

Lambley

S. Tyne Trail

Eals

Slaggyford

Kirkhaugh

0 1 2 3 4 5km

© Crown Copyright.

Alston

Bleagate

Garrigill

Ashgill Force

P.W.

Black Burn

P.W.

Tyne Head

S. Tyne

Cross Fell

Great Dun Fell

Tees

16

Cross Fell to Haltwhistle.

From the wild moorlands the path dives for the verdant valleys, following the river down to Garrigill, passing little-known but spectacular Ashgill Force on the way.

The path on to Alston could be the Pennine Way, on the south bank to Bleagate, but a route along the north bank is suggested.

Alston offers a youth hostel, shops, inns, buses, etc, as well as being an attractive town.

Users of the Pennine Way from Alston to Greenhead, do not see the best of the valley: it meanders along the boggy edges of the moors, trying to avoid roads, but succeeding in missing the best scenery too! The track of the old railway offers a better trail as far as Lambley, whilst lanes and footpaths along the east flank of the valley offer a genuinely superior alternative.

Along the way you pass Kirkhaugh, with its tiny church with needle spire: A different, but still elegant style of architecture is shown by the 110' high Lambley viaduct.

Further downriver, paths take you past Featherstone Castle or Bellister Castle, with parkland, woods and farmland on the way to Haltwhistle.

Haltwhistle offers a full range of facilities, buses and trains included, and a choice of onward itineraries.

Kirkhaugh:

17

Long Preamble: to Tyne Head via Cross Fell

from Garrigill 22.8 km (14 miles)
from Dufton 16.0 km (10 miles)

Tyne Head is such a mediocre starting point for such a great river system that some will look for a more fitting or impressive starting point. Black Beck, a tributary, rises high on Cross Fell. This, as the highest point in the Pennines (893 metres, 2930 ft) fits the bill as a starting point. But the Black Burn is sadly lacking in terms of public paths.

A compromise is to start from Cross Fell having walked up the Pennine Way from Garrigill (or Dufton) then follow the Pennine Way south over the Dun Fells and down the bridle-way into the upper Tees valley, and round to Tyne Head:

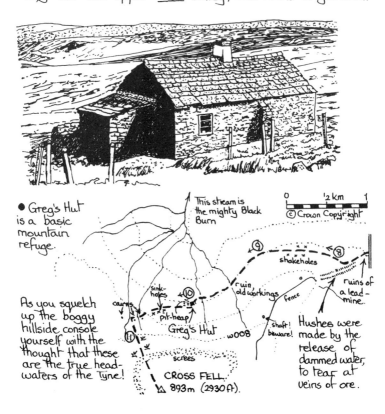

● Greg's Hut is a basic mountain refuge.

This stream is the mighty Black Burn

0   ½ km   1
© Crown Copyright

As you squelch up the boggy hillside console yourself with the thought that these are the true head-waters of the Tyne!

shakeholes

ruin old workings

sink-holes

cairns

pit-heap

Greg's Hut

w008

shaft! beware!

ruins of a lead-mine.

fence

Hushes were made by the release of dammed water, to tear at veins of ore.

screes

CROSS FELL.
△ 893 m (2930 ft).

18

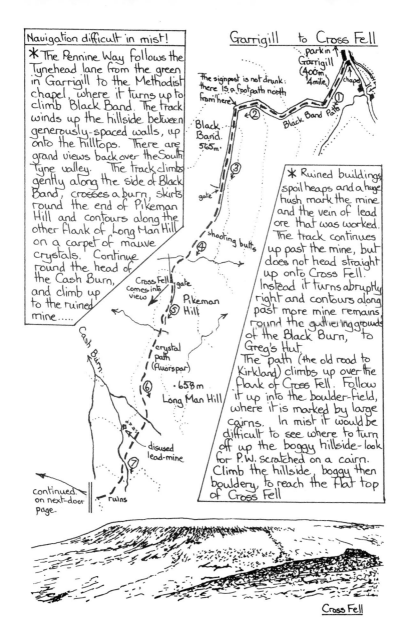

Navigation difficult in mist!

*The Pennine Way follows the Tynehead lane from the green in Garrigill to the Methodist chapel, where it turns up to climb Black Band. The track winds up the hillside between generously-spaced walls, up onto the hilltops. There are grand views back over the South Tyne valley. The track climbs gently along the side of Black Band, crosses a burn, skirts round the end of Pikeman Hill and contours along the other flank of Long Man Hill on a carpet of mauve crystals. Continue round the head of the Cash Burn, and climb up to the ruined mine.....

Garrigill to Cross Fell

park in Garrigill (400m, ¼ mile)

chapel

The signpost is not drunk: there is a footpath north from here.

Black Band Path

①

②

Black Band. 565m.

③

gate

shooting butts

④

Cross Fell comes into view

gate

⑤ Pikeman Hill

Cash Burn

crystal path (Fluorspar)

⑥ ·658m Long Man Hill

disused lead-mine

⑦

continued. on next-door page.

ruins

*Ruined buildings spoil heaps and a huge hush mark the mine and the vein of lead ore that was worked. The track continues up past the mine, but does not head straight up onto Cross Fell. Instead it turns abruptly right and contours along past more mine remains round the gathering grounds of the Black Burn, to Greg's Hut. The path (the old road to Kirkland) climbs up over the flank of Cross Fell. Follow it up into the boulder-field, where it is marked by large cairns. In mist it would be difficult to see where to turn off up the boggy hillside- look for P.W. scratched on a cairn. Climb the hillside, boggy then bouldery, to reach the flat top of Cross Fell

Cross Fell

- Cross Fell is the highest of the Pennines, at almost 3000' one of the highest hills in England. It gathers weather from both east and west: it can be fierce!

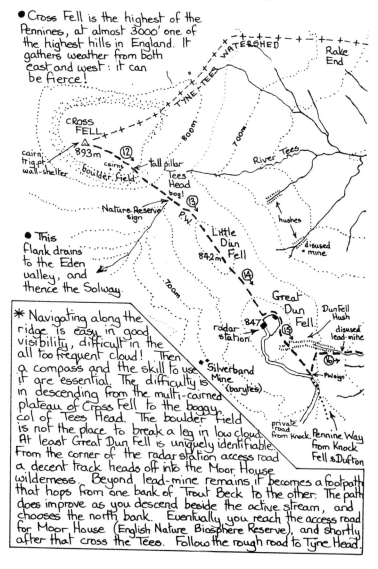

- This flank drains to the Eden valley, and thence the Solway.

* Navigating along the ridge is easy in good visibility, difficult in the all too frequent cloud! Then a compass and the skill to use it are essential. The difficulty is in descending from the multi-cairned plateau of Cross Fell to the boggy col of Tees Head. The boulder field is not the place to break a leg in low cloud. At least Great Dun Fell is uniquely identifiable. From the corner of the radar station access road a decent track heads off into the Moor House wilderness. Beyond lead-mine remains it becomes a footpath that hops from one bank of Trout Beck to the other. The path does improve as you descend beside the active stream, and chooses the north bank. Eventually you reach the access road for Moor House (English Nature Biosphere Reserve), and shortly after that cross the Tees. Follow the rough road to Tyne Head.

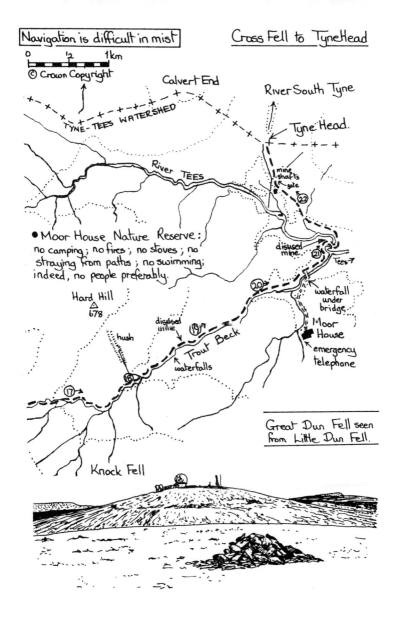

Navigation is difficult in mist

0   ½   1km
© Crown Copyright

Calvert End

River South Tyne

TYNE-TEES WATERSHED

Tyne Head.

River TEES

mine shafts
gate

22

disused mine

• Moor House Nature Reserve:
no camping; no fires; no stoves; no
straying from paths; no swimming;
indeed, no people preferably.

21

Tees →

20

Hard Hill
△ 678

disused mine

19

Trout Beck

hush

waterfalls

waterfall under bridge

Moor House

emergency telephone

18

17

Great Dun Fell seen
from Little Dun Fell.

Knock Fell

21

Short Preamble: to Tyne Head

from Garrigill 7km, (4½ miles)
from Hill House 3.5km (2¼ miles)

✳ There is only one public right-of-way to Tyne Head, the valley road from Garrigill that continues beyond Hill House, soon becoming a farm road that climbs up beside the South Tyne to the col of Tyne Head.
  A map is given on page 25.

A map is given on page 25.

• The road goes on, over into the Tees catchment area, to Moor House. A track leaves it to wind up beside Trout Beck to the Pennine ridge between Knock Fell and Great Dun Fell, from where a road drops down to Dufton. You can reach Tyne Head that way — but that is the Long Preamble on the previous page!

The first bridge:

Public transport to Garrigill is sparse to non-existent. Buses serve Alston. Cars can reach to just above Hill House.

22

Tyne Head.

The official "source" of the South Tyne is unspectacular. There is no gushing spring, no gaping crack in a cliff. It is just a bog. It is not even on a mountain top, just a col between rounded hills. Worse, there are much higher tributaries: Black Burn rises high up on Cross Fell. Indeed, the Ordnance Survey shows the Black Burn in preference to the South Tyne on its 1:1 000 000 map of Great Britain. But the dale does lead inexorably up to this gap between Round Hill and Tynehead Fell, and this boggy gap is a gateway between the great river systems of the Tyne and the Tees — the latter already a river just 500 metres down the slope beyond the col. It is almost a meeting place of the northern counties of England: within 10 kilometres (six miles) you can be in Northumberland or the old North Riding of Yorkshire; County Durham is just 2½ kilometres (1½ miles) away; Westmoreland is just across the Tees. Tyne Head itself is within Cumberland.

But that is to over-emphasise its importance. It really is just a boggy col at the top of a valley. Even the hardy miners have given up their pits on the hills round about, and have left it all to the birds. The river improves rapidly as you leave Tyne Head behind, being fed by the boggy sponges of Round Hill and Tynehead Fell. So do not hang around here. There are much nicer places to be, down the Tyne.

23

Tyne Head to Garrigill.   (8km, 5miles)

✳ A good, mostly metalled track runs alongside the river down the narrow rift between Round Hill and Tynehead Fell. Cross the first arched bridge, by a large modern barn, and follow the track as it contours away from the river. Go past Dorth Gill to the public road, and on along to Hill House. If there is still no sign of the footpath down to the bridge, descend by the zig-zag. Cross the bridge to Hole House.
Follow indistinct paths northwards, passing derelict mine-heaps. The paths become clear, and waymarked, over stiles and footbridges, as you approach Ashgillside.

There the path has been diverted, through a gate and past the east side of the first house by a series of stiles. Go between the other houses and a stile shows the way beside a large shed. Continue over the fields to Pasture Houses. You cross the lane below the row of houses, onto a farm-track. Turn left through a gate onto a descending path that drops gently towards Garrigill, emerging at the bridge in the village.

Hole House

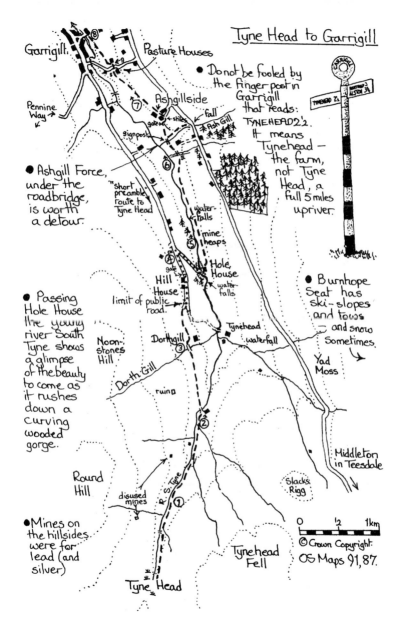

Tyne Head to Garrigill

Garrigill.

Pasture Houses

Ashgillside

Pennine Way

• Do not be fooled by the finger post in Garrigill that reads: TYNEHEAD 2½. It means Tynehead — the farm, not Tyne Head, a full 5 miles upriver.

GARRIGILL / TYNEHEAD 2½ / MIDDLETON 3 / ALSTON 3¾

fall
gate + stiles
Ash Gill fall
signpost

• Ashgill Force, under the roadbridge, is worth a detour.

⑦

⑥

"short preamble route to Tyne Head"

water-falls

mine heaps

⑤

④ gate

Hill House

Hole House

water-falls

limit of public road.

• Passing Hole House the young river South Tyne shows a glimpse of the beauty to come as it rushes down a curving wooded gorge.

Noon-stones Hill

Dorthgill ③

Dorth Gill

ruin

Tynehead

waterfall

• Burnhope Seat has ski-slopes and tows — and snow sometimes.

Yad Moss

Round Hill

disused mines

os Tyne

① ②

Middleton in Teesdale

Slacks Rigg

• Mines on the hillsides were for lead (and silver)

Tyne Head

Tynehead Fell

0   ½   1km

© Crown Copyright.
OS Maps 91, 87.

Ashgill Force.

is worth the digression, or even a visit in its own right. The fall tumbles splendidly into a rocky canyon. A path goes round behind the curtain of water on a deep ledge – for careful explorers only! It is much finer than many better-known falls, and easy to get to: the Alston-Middleton road soars over the top!

● Below the fall can be seen traces of the old lead-mines. This was a scene of industry in the 19th century, as a very profitable lead-mine emerged here, large enough to use a horse tramway and profitable enough to buy the whole estate. Paths lead up to the rockface, and one fissure offers a route up, to join the path up to the road beside the bridge. This is a good place to explore.

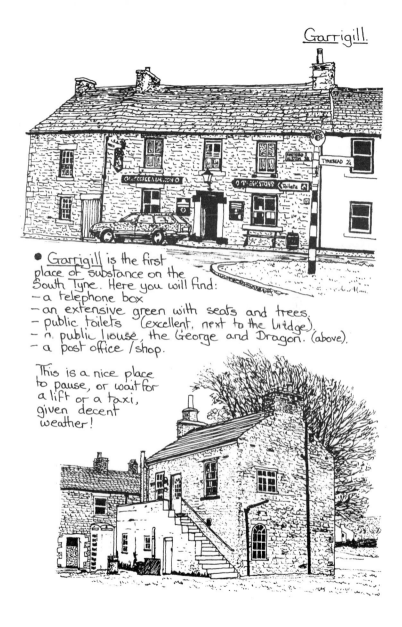

● <u>Garrigill</u> is the first
place of substance on the
South Tyne. Here you will find:
- a telephone box
- an extensive green with seats and trees.
- public toilets (excellent, next to the bridge).
- a public house, the George and Dragon. (above).
- a post office / shop.

This is a nice place
to pause, or wait for
a lift or a taxi,
given decent
weather!

27

Garrigill to Alston

6.7 km (4 miles) of field paths
(14.2 km (9 miles) there and back.

✳ Cross the South Tyne in Garrigill and follow the lane along past Beldy Chapel (there Garrigill Burn, confined to a culvert by the lead miners, now enjoys daylight again, tumbling down a 'restored' waterfall above the road bridge). Continue past the cemetery. A gate on the left opens onto a diagonal path down across a pasture to a gap. There a shelf carries the path along well above the riverside meadows. (Avoid an obvious track that descends to old lead-mines.) The way-marked path goes on along the top of wooded limestone cliffs past the farm at Low Craig to Low Sillyhall. There the Pennine Way comes up from the footbridge. Continue across the fields to Bleagate, where you go down through the farmyard and turn right. Follow the Pennine Way on by a series of stiles and gates towards Alston. The Black Burn valley stretches away to the south-west, with Cross Fell looming up on the skyline. Down below the path the South Tyne wanders northwards. You cross Nattrass Gill by a footbridge, and gently rise onto the tree-clad bluffs — The Firs — overlooking the river. Approach Alston past the Youth Hostel, just before Alston Bridge, go down the steps to the road, and walk into town.

Riverbank walk
by Low Skydes.

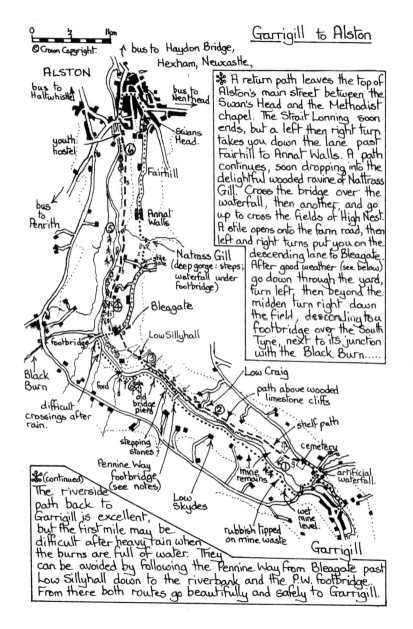

0   ½   1km
© Crown Copyright.

↑ bus to Haydon Bridge,
Hexham, Newcastle,

ALSTON

bus to Haltwhistle ↑

youth hostel

bus to Nenthead

Swans Head.

Fairhill

bus to Penrith

Annat Walls

Natrass Gill
(deep gorge: steps;
waterfall under
footbridge)

stile gate

Bleagate

Low Sillyhall

footbridge

Black Burn

difficult crossings after rain.

ford

old bridge piers

stepping stones

Pennine Way footbridge
(see notes)

Low Skydes

Low Craig

path above wooded limestone cliffs

shelf path

cemetery

artificial waterfall

mine remains

rubbish tipped on mine waste

wet mine level

Garrigill

✳ A return path leaves the top of Alston's main street between the Swan's Head and the Methodist chapel. The Strait Lonning soon ends, but a left then right turn takes you down the lane past Fairhill to Annat Walls. A path continues, soon dropping into the delightful wooded ravine of Nattrass Gill. Cross the bridge over the waterfall, then another, and go up to cross the fields of High Nest. A stile opens onto the farm road, then left and right turns put you on the descending lane to Bleagate. After good weather (see below) go down through the yard, turn left, then beyond the midden turn right down the field, descending to a footbridge over the South Tyne, next to its junction with the Black Burn.....

✳ (continued)
The riverside path back to Garrigill is excellent, but the first mile may be difficult after heavy rain when the burns are full of water. They can be avoided by following the Pennine Way from Bleagate past Low Sillyhall down to the riverbank and the P.W. footbridge. From there both routes go beautifully and safely to Garrigill.

29

Alston

• Alston vies with Buxton in the Peak District for the title of highest market town in England. According to Ordnance Survey maps Buxton lies between 290m and 320m above sea level, whereas Alston is between 270m at Alston Bridge (below) and 330m at the top of the town, so you can take your choice. Certainly Alston is steeper, with its cobbled main streets reaching up into the Pennine sky. It is this unusual steepness which is at the root of Alston's siting: unseen by today's visitors a burn hurtles down the hillside under the eastern side of the town, now channelled away out of sight. It powered a succession of mills, from the forge at the top of the town, down through the High Mill (corn), a sawmill, and finally the low Mill. One branch of the millrace runs down under Alston's main road – Front Street – for a short way.

The River Nent added its share to Alston's water power, with a large worsted mill below the town.

Alston Bridge.

The market cross. (1765, but much rebuilt because of runaway lorries!)

But now Alston is less industrial, and has quite consciously set out to attract a tourist trade and to cater all year for escapees from the rat race. Many have discovered that these northern dales offer a different quality of life for those who are not tied to cities and conurbations by their work. These two foci have given Alston its own distinctive flavour amongst northern towns, a certain charm, and a variety of facilities. These include a bank; a fish-and-chip shop; a specialist bakery; an outdoor pursuits shop; a variety of other shops; cafés; teashops; hotels; restaurants; public houses; churches. There is a variety of accommodation, including a youth hostel (by Alston Bridge). Buses connect Alston with Haltwhistle via Slaggyford, Lambley and Coanwood, and connect with trains on the Newcastle-Carlisle line. Buses also run (less often) to Hexham and Newcastle, and over Hartside Pass to Penrith. In summer there may be infrequent services over the watershed to Middleton-in-Teesdale.

The railway to Haltwhistle has gone, but a narrow gauge line offers a change of mode for those in the mood:

South Tynedale Railway.

Alston station, with a diesel engine shunting.

Polish industrial
steam at Alston: Naklo.

• The branch-line up the South Tyne valley from Haltwhistle to Alston opened in 1852. It carried a fair coal traffic from the Lambley Colliery Railway, and miraculously continued to carry passengers until 1976. Its survival for so long, after so many lines had closed in the Beeching era, was due to conditions on winter roads: a replacement service of buses could not be reliably guaranteed until the new bridge and road were opened between Lambley and Coanwood. It had been widely reported that the cost of keeping the line open was equivalent to providing each passenger with a chauffeur-driven Rolls Royce. Such an exchange was not, of course, offered: after closure passengers had to make do with the bus service to Haltwhistle.

The track was lifted, and Alston station lost its train-shed. The valley echoed no more to the sounds of passing trains.

But then the South Tynedale Railway started up. The prospects for success for a narrow-gauge tourist railway up in remote Tynedale seemed small, but by 1983 they were running trains again. Gradually the line has been extended: Alston station; to Gilderdale (the County boundary); to Kirkhaugh. The railway hopes to reach Slaggyford.

Trains run at Spring holiday and summer weekends, hauled by narrow-gauge steam or diesel locomotives. Works trains, such as that shown heading for Kirkhaugh station, may run at other times too. The sight, sounds and smells of railway operation have returned to the valley.

• The trackbed is paralleled by a footpath, — the South Tyne Trail — from Alston to Lambley.

Alston to Kirkhaugh: 4·4km (2¾ miles) beside the railway.
3·4km (2 miles) by riverside path/lane.
6·5km (4 miles) by the Pennine Way.

There are three good routes north from Alston down the valley:
the Pennine Way tries very hard to avoid roads, and wanders along
the mid-slopes of the valley wall; the riverside lane is superb
when there is no traffic; the path beside the railway, the South
Tyne Trail is probably the best, offering better views of the river
and the valley than the wandering Pennine Way.

---

* From the signpost at Alston Townfoot follow the Hexham
road down to cross the Nent, and turn in at the station. The
footpath starts beyond the level crossing, along the top of the
wall above the rushing South Tyne. Beyond the carriage
and engine sheds the path swaps to the east side of the line.
It crosses the river and continues along embankments and
through cuttings. Views of the river and valley are excellent.
Gilderdale Halt (inaccessible by road) comes just before the county
boundary at Gilderdale Burn Bridge, with Kirkhaugh station just
a kilometre further on. Leave the station there by the footpath
down the hill to the footbridge. Cross the river and follow
the track round the north side of the field to the lane. Walk
back to visit the little church of Kirkhaugh (if you want!).

---

*1. The short route also starts along the Hexham road, past
the station. A little way up the hill a footpath sign points the
way to Paddy's Well steps. The path goes down past a clutter
of buildings to the riverbank, just by the railway bridge. Follow
the bank along, until the U-bend of the river forces you up
the steps to meet the lane above. Follow the lane down to
Randalholme, cross Ayle Burn into Northumberland and
continue below Kirkside Wood to Kirkhaugh.

---

*2. The Pennine Way route crosses Alston Bridge (south of
Townfoot), then turns north along field paths to Harbut Lodge,
where it shuffles up to the main road (A689). It escapes
beyond Harbut Law onto the hillside. A long diversion—the
original route—is avoided by a long-established short-cut (by
a series of ladder stiles) down to the footbridge over Gilderdale Burn. The footpath climbs the flanks of the moors,
to loop past Whitley Castle — a Roman fort on the Maiden
Way. The path drops down towards Castle Nook, where it
takes avoiding action—across the little stream into a wood,
to reach the road by the telephone box. A diagonal field-
path takes you on past Dyke House to Kirkhaugh station.

Return could be by any route — or by bus or even train!

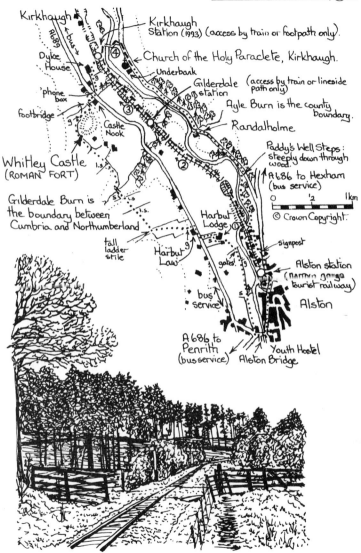

Kirkhaugh

Kirkhaugh Station (1993) (access by train or footpath only).

Dyke House

Church of the Holy Paraclete, Kirkhaugh.

Underbank

Gilderdale station (access by train or lineside path only)

'phone box

Ayle Burn is the county boundary.

footbridge

Randalholme

Castle Nook

Paddy's Well Steps: steeply down through wood.

Whitley Castle (ROMAN FORT)

A686 to Hexham (bus service)

Gilderdale Burn is the boundary between Cumbria and Northumberland

0   ·2   1km

© Crown Copyright.

tall ladder stile

Harbut Lodge

signpost

Harbut Law

gates

Alston station (narrow gauge tourist railway)

bus service

Alston

A686 to Penrith (bus service)

Alston Bridge

Youth Hostel

● The lane on the east bank runs next to the river, with grand views of the fells to the west on the open patches (as at Kirkside-above), or rather more localised views in the beech woods that stretch down to the riverbank. (below).

- <u>Kirkhaugh</u>: the little Church of the Holy Paraclete is in a beautiful spot on the river meadows. Its design, with an unusually slender spire and tall lancet windows, reflects the taste of the Victorian vicar who had it rebuilt in 1868-9. It replaced an older building of plainer design, which had large square windows to make good use of the limited light in the valley. The 13th century west window was incorporated into the rebuild.

- <u>Kirkhaugh Bridge</u> links the church bank (Kirkside) with the scattered farms of Kirkhaugh on the west bank.

Kirkhaugh to Slaggyford.   4.2km (2½ miles) of lanes and paths.
or 4.5km (2¾ miles) by Pennine Way.

● The massive piers of the footbridge below Barhaugh are a
reminder that this rural valley had an industrial phase – pits in
the Barhaugh area.

● The South Tyne at Thompson's Well Bridge
can be a trickle amongst boulders
– or a torrent that grinds them!

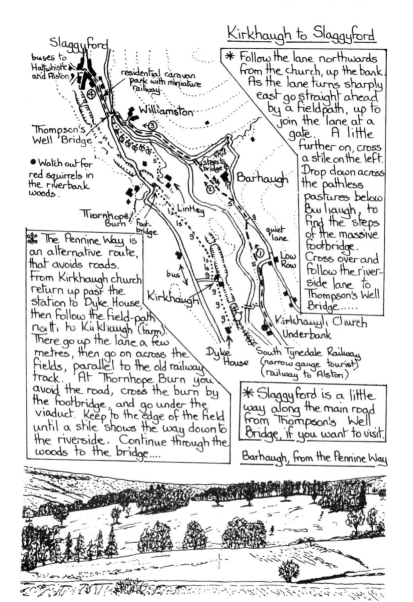

Kirkhaugh to Slaggyford

Slaggyford

buses to Halfwhistle and Alston

residential caravan park with miniature railway

Williamston

Thompson's Well Bridge

● Watch out for red squirrels in the riverbank woods.

Thornhope Burn Foot-bridge

LinHey

steps to bridge

Barhaugh

quiet lane

Low Row

❀ The Pennine Way is an alternative route, that avoids roads. From Kirkhaugh church return up past the station to Dyke House, then follow the field-path north to Kirkhaugh (farm). There go up the lane a few metres, then go on across the fields, parallel to the old railway track. At Thornhope Burn you avoid the road, cross the burn by the footbridge, and go under the viaduct. Keep to the edge of the field until a stile shows the way down to the riverside. Continue through the woods to the bridge....

bus

Kirkhaugh

Dyke House

Kirkhaugh Church Underbank

South Tynedale Railway (narrow gauge tourist) (railway to Alston)

✳ Follow the lane northwards from the church, up the bank. As the lane turns sharply east go straight ahead by a fieldpath, up to join the lane at a gate. A little further on, cross a stile on the left. Drop down across the pathless pastures below Barhaugh, to find the steps of the massive footbridge. Cross over and follow the riverside lane to Thompson's Well Bridge.....

✳ Slaggyford is a little way along the main road from Thompson's Well Bridge, if you want to visit.

Barhaugh, from the Pennine Way

Slaggyford to Lambley

9.5km (6 miles); footpaths, lanes and views
or 6.3km (4 miles) of old railway line.

Looking back from the shelf over Parson Shields to Thornhope Fell.

❀ The South Tyne Trail provides an alternative route, using the bed of
the old Haltwhistle-Alston railway from Slaggyford station almost to
Lambley station – a private residence. As with all railway routes it is
gently graded and a touch monotonous. Unlike many, it suffers from
disturbed drains and is vilely boggy in places. It is better than the Pennine
Way, which follows the Maiden Way dully along the foot of the moors.

Down in the woods: the descent to Snope Burn.

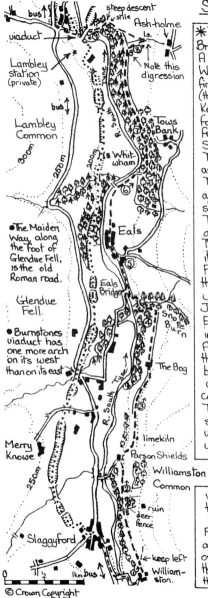

Slaggyford to Lambley.

⁎ The lane from Thompson's Well
Bridge goes to the farm, Williamston.
A track heads up onto the flank of
Williamston Common. After the
first rise keep left on a faint path
(the track continues up to a ruin).
Keep above the tree belt (except
for a short section between deer
fences), and descend to Parson
Shields.

This, with its large sheds, can be
avoided on the east side.

The path climbs again, up past
a ruin and a limekiln, onto a
shelf. The views are superb.
The shelf path gains a wall,
and takes you to The Bog.
This farm, more attractive than
its name, is served by a lane.
Follow it north, and down
the zig-zags in the wood to
cross Snope Burn.
Join the lane at attractive
Eals Bridge, and walk along
into Eals.

A rough track continues across
the river meadows, to a footbridge (useful for shortening
circular walks). A footpath
continues by the riverbank to
Towsbank Wood. Cross the
stream (footbridge) and climb
up steeply in the wood, following
waymarks (if any!).

There are fine views back
upriver. The path levels
out, and soon follows the
valley rim along at the top of
the wood. Watch for Lambley
Viaduct, down the valley.
A digression is required, up
a path towards Ash-holme,
over a stile and back to join
the footpath descending to
the footbridge at Lambley.

41

Slaggyford to Lambley

The routes described in the book make use of many of the bridges over the South Tyne. But here are three that you will not cross (except on diversions), although you may venture onto some for the views.

● Right: Eals Bridge carries the road between the hamlet of Eals and the scattered settlement of Knarsdale.

● The footbridge that carries the path from Eals to Whitwham links a flat watermeadow on the east bank to a rugged wall of rock on the west side. When the river is running strongly this is an exciting place to be.

• The railway viaduct at Lambley carried the Alston branch railway from 1852 until closure in 1976. For 16 months before the viaduct opened the railway was linked to the national system only by the network of colliery lines that stretched from Lambley colliery to Brampton. These little-known lines — the Brampton Railway - closed in 1953. It seems odd to think of Lambley as a railway junction and industrial centre as it slumbers in post-industrial isolation.

Lumps of masonry began to flake off the viaduct in the 1990s, rendering the attached footbridge unsafe. A new footbridge has been built (1992), a few metres down-river. Extensive restoration work in 1996 has allowed the viaduct to be re-opened for pedestrians.

43

Lambley to Haltwhistle   8.3km (5¼ miles) of riverside and fields.

● Lambley cannot boast many facilities for the walker. But there is a telephone box in the hamlet, and on the main road up the hill there is a bus service to Alston and Haltwhistle.

✳ A path runs behind the houses on the east side of the street, and steps lead down to the old colliery line. Cross over and descend the zig-zag path under the trees. Branch left before the viaduct. (The other branch goes under the viaduct, below the old station – now private – then up to join the railway and the South Tyne Trail). Your path goes down to the footbridge, just downstream from the 110 feet high viaduct.
Cross the river. The path heads away downstream, then loops away from the river towards the railway embankment. (An alternative route diverges here – see next page).
A sharp left turn by the buildings and a path down across the fields takes you back to the riverside, which continues to Coanwood Bridge.

● Coanwood road-bridge was the key to closure of the Alston Railway in 1976. The railway had been kept open, despite losing money, because the roads across the moors to Alston were frequently blocked by winter snows. But the new 'valley' road via Coanwood and Lambley solved that problem, and the railway closed.

✳ The path crosses the road and continues downstream through Featherstone Park. River erosion of the banks is very active, so watch your step! Pass – at a distance - Featherstone Castle, and go on to the footbridge. Cross over to the west bank and turn right. The path goes muddily along the bank, under the trees, and emerges on the lane just above Featherstone Bridge. Go down and look at the bridge, which is asymmetrical to suit the terrain.
Climb back up the lane for a few metres, and turn right down the farm track to Wydon Eals. The foot-path turns left at the farm, and climbs the bank to get above the trees. A succession of stiles and gates indicates the way across the ridge to Wydon, where the farm track provides a clear route onwards. Opposite Bellister Castle cross the Tipalt Burn by the footbridge and follow the lane into Haltwhistle.

Lambley to Haltwhistle

Haltwhistle (town)

buses and trains to Carlisle.

buses and trains to Hexham and Newcastle

Wydon

Bellister Castle (National Trust).

0   ½   1 Km
© Crown Copyright.

Wydon Eals

Broom-house Common

Park Village

Lynnshield

Feather-stone Castle (private)

Rowfoot phone

ex P.o.W camp

f.b.

car-park

bus

Coanwood.

phone

old station

bus

Lambley Viaduct

steps

✳ Another route from Coanwood to Haltwhistle (unsafe in mist). Climb up past the site of the old station and go round to the carpark where the old line meets the new road. Follow the rim of the cutting northwards, presently bearing right to a footbridge, then across fields to Rowfoot. Follow the road down to cross the Park Burn. A stile gives onto a faint path. Climb up in a gap in the trees to reach Lynnshield. A stile behind the barn gives access to a path along the rim of the Park Burn gorge. Follow it out onto the moor. Turn north at the wall, and cross the moor. You should meet the railway and ladder-stiles, just south of Bellister Castle (still hidden by the terrain). Climb up the bank and go along above the trees to find a stile and descending path. Cross the fields below and turn right along the lane to the old bridge.

45

● <u>Featherstone Castle</u>. The Featherstonehaughs built a tower here in the 12th century. Parts were incorporated into an L-shaped tower in 1330. The 'castle' was extended greatly after the main danger (Scots invasion) was over, after the Union. The castellated additions – including the garden wall - neatly matched the old tower. It is still occupied and is PRIVATE. It is situated in beautiful parkland, which housed a prisoner-of-war camp during the Second World War.

• <u>Featherstone Bridge</u> dates from 1778. It looks distinctly odd, as the angle of the parapet is offset from the keystone.

• The local castles are reputedly haunted, Featherstone by a ghostly bridal party. After the local heiress, Abigal Featherstone-haugh, was married, jealous loser Hugh Ridley ambushed the wedding party. Abigal was killed trying to stop the fight, where-upon Hugh Ridley put a period to his existence......
At Bellister legend recalls an elderly wandering minstrel who was suspected of being a spy. He fled, and was brought down by the castle hounds. He is said to appear as the Grey Man.

• <u>Bellister Castle</u>, in the Tyne Gap, was fortified early. A sturdy bastle, with a motte and ditch was built by the Blenkinsopps. A castellated farmhouse was added later. Now the ruined bastle is owned by the National Trust and can be visited by prior appointment.

47

Haltwhistle

- Haltwhistle is not just a railway station. It is a quiet little Northumberland market town, with a main street of shops and banks, a very old church, a suburb of housing and a remnant of industry. Coal used to be its staple industry, with a colliery up beside the Haltwhistle Burn, and a long seam up in the fells on the south of the South Tyne. The latter is still productive, and coal from Plenmeller Common comes down on a conveyor to cross the Tyne to a railhead just east of the town.
The Haltwhistle Burn was the scene of much other industry: mills for wool, timber and corn used waterpower before coal, and there was a tile works, a brewery, a gasworks and coke ovens as well, all served by a railway siding. Even now there is a transport company based there.
When the railway came to Haltwhistle in 1838, followed by the Alston branch in 1852, the town became a significant railhead for the area. The branch succumbed to a new road in 1976, but Haltwhistle is still an important stop for all trains on the main line.

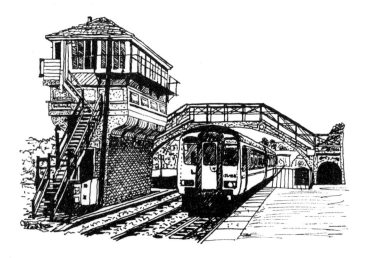

- The North Eastern Railway signal box is unusual in being raised on a narrow plinth. This gave it a good view of the main lines, the branch and the goods yards. It has now lost its function, but remains as a listed building.

48

Haltwhistle is a point of choice for walkers travelling long-distance, down the South Tyne. Here you decide what kind of walking you want tomorrow. There are four main choices:

① Keep company with the river, crossing back to the south bank for a stroll along riverside lanes, meadows and woods to Bardon Mill.

② Catch a train or a bus west to Brampton, where you can head back east, passing Lanercost Priory and keeping company with Hadrian's Wall.

③ Catch a bus west to Greenhead (where there is a youth hostel) and then walk east along the Wall.

④ Walk up the Haltwhistle Burn to meet the Roman Wall at Cawfields milecastle, and head either east or west along the Wall.

Your choices will be influenced by a variety of factors:

- where you aim to stay the next night (there are youth hostels at Greenhead and at Once Brewed.)
- availability of transport – the valley bus service is useful and runs all year.
  - the Hadrian's Wall bus services are infrequent and seasonal.
  - not all trains stop at Bardon Mill.

- historical interest – Hadrian's Wall is a big lure
  - so are Lanercost Priory & Birdoswald.

- walking quality – Brampton to Greenhead has a high proportion of road-walking.
  - the Roman Wall is rugged.
  - the valley route is easy.

- the weather – Hadrian's Wall can be bleakly miserable if the weather is unkind.

- purism – some walkers will not catch buses or trains!

So Haltwhistle is a good place to sit in a café or a bed-and-breakfast and read the chapters about the valley route and the Wall route, and make some choices.

Chapter Two: The South Tyne and Allen Banks.

From Haltwhistle to Bardon Mill a succession of quiet lanes and field paths provides a gentle alternative to the rigours of the exposed Hadrian's Wall route (Chapter 3). The route provides a variety of wildlife habitats — lanes, hedges, fields, and plantations, so take binoculars with you — and historical interest in the fortified farm at Willimoteswick.

Bardon Mill is a good starting point for an excursion to Vindolanda, climbing the valley to the fascinating Roman fort, town and museum, with a return route over the high ridge of Barcombe.

Cupola Bridge

Haltwhistle to Hexham, with digressions.

Allen Banks have long had a deserved reputation for their beauty, and can be followed up to Staward and back, with walks in the woods and beside the rushing River Allen.
East of the Allen high field-paths provide excellent views of the River South Tyne on the way to Haydon Bridge.

A circular walk from Haydon Bridge visits the woodlands on the southern flanks of the South Tyne, and passes Langley Castle.

The South Tyne at Haydon Bridge.

Roads follow both banks to the east of Haydon Bridge, so the walker either grits his teeth and heads for Newbrough in company with the traffic, or escapes to the hills. The described route climbs up from Haydon Bridge to visit the old church of St. Cuthbert, then crosses Haydon Fell to reach the Stanegate. This Roman road, now a lane, leads down towards Newbrough.
A riverside path starts again, and is followed along the north bank below the slopes of Warden Hill to West Boat. Just up the lane, and well worth a visit, is the delightful church at Warden.
The south bank of the South Tyne is followed by a footpath to the river's confluence with the North Tyne. The new river — the Tyne — is followed downstream to the interesting town of Hexham.

Haltwhistle to Bardon Mill

9.4km (5¼ miles) of lanes and farm tracks across river meadows.

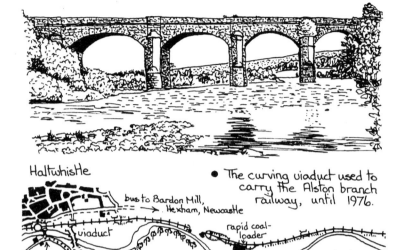

Haltwhistle

- The curving viaduct used to carry the Alston branch railway, until 1976.

bus to Bardon Mill, Hexham, Newcastle

viaduct
rapid coal-loader
bridge
Plenmeller
West Unthank
East Unthank ⑤
plastic bottle factory
Unthank Hall
coal conveyor
© Crown Copyright

✳ Just east of Haltwhistle station a minor road dives under the tracks and crosses a ramshackle bridge to the south bank. Turn left and follow the lane up to join the old line that used to sweep round over the viaduct. Go under it and past the junction from the bottle factory, and through the hamlet of Plenmeller. Turn left along the lane towards Unthank, a delightful avenue of trees culminating in a fine colour group of trees as you skirt round the Hall.....

- Unthank Hall (long before the current rebuild) was probably the birthplace of Bishop Ridley, burnt by Mary Tudor in 1555 for adhering to the newfangled Protestant faith.

Just beyond the Hall, by its defunct walled garden, the Tyne is crossed by a coal conveyor linking the revived mine on Plenmeller Common to the railway.

*... Beyond Unthank Hall the lane continues to East Unthank. Just before it, you follow a track left down onto the haughs, and walk along below the woods to Shankfoot. There you climb up again to a higher level, where a rough track heads eastwards above the bank, close to the river. Perhaps rabbits will scatter ahead of you, like a bow-wave as they dive for their warren. Haughstrother Wood provides rather different scenery for a little while, then you continue above the bank to Oadhall Mill (pass through the gates and north of the cottage). The track curves up the bank towards the gaunt outline of Willimontswick, where you meet a metalled lane to take you down towards Bardon Mill. A long footbridge crosses the river to the village.

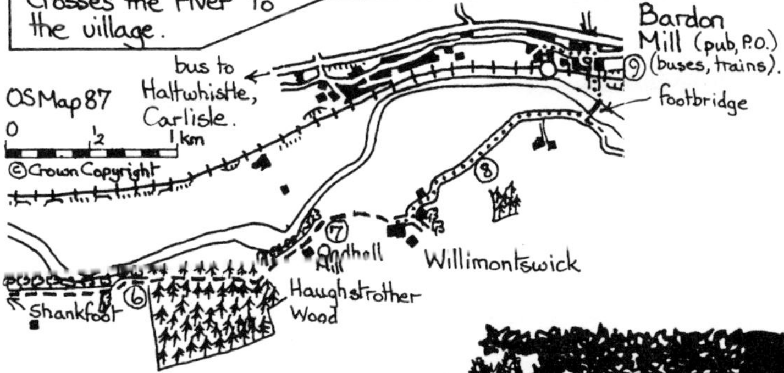

Bardon Mill (pub, P.O.)
(buses, trains).

bus to Haltwhistle, Carlisle.

footbridge

OS Map 87

0   ½   1 km
© Crown Copyright

Shankfoot

Oadhall

Haughstrother Wood

Willimontswick

Approaching Unthank Hall.

● <u>Willimoteswick</u> is a farm with a difference. This seat of the Ridley family during the Middle Ages is still a working farm (and PRIVATE!). But it incorporates the remains of the old border fortress. The massive gate-house guards the north-east entrance to the farm-yard, while remains of the tower are built into the manor-house. The whole stands proudly on the slopes above the Tyne, reminding all who pass along the valley of the long history of Border raiding. The Ridleys were not all saints, and participated fully in the local sport.

● The length of the <u>footbridge</u> at Bardon Mill, and the broken-down state of the ford (at the time of writing), bear witness that the Tyne is not always placid, gentle and inviting.

Bardon Mill

• Hospitality in the village is provided by the <u>Bowes Hotel</u>. There is also a post office and store. A roughly hourly bus-service along the valley supplements the rather sparse train service.

• <u>Bardon Mill</u> is another of the industrial villages dotted along the Tyne corridor. The coal that outcrops along the valley sides, together with water and good transport, meant that the industrial revolution would not give this valley a miss. The industry has not all disappeared under a cloak of scrubby woodland, as so often in the north of England.

Here in Bardon Mill the brickworks is still active. The kiln is used largely to fire large urns and planters for the gardens of post-industrial Tyneside.

Bardon Mill and Vindolanda. 7.4 or 6.2km (4½ or 4 miles)

* The footpath leaves Bardon Mill past the kiln, and climbs up onto the embankment of the busy A69. It continues on the other side, entering a field to skirt 'Bankhead' then using the farm access road. Turn right up the lane past 'Cragside' and down to the junction in a dip. Keep straight on, up the hill to the corner, where a wall-stile gives access to a field-path. Climb diagonally up the hill-side under the wires to a stile in the corner overlooking the Chineley Burn gorge. Head north, dropping gently down on the old cart-track to the bridge over the Bean Burn below Low Fogrigg.

Follow the path up to the right of the solitary house, and continue to flank the Chineley burn valley, crossing a series of stiles. Just before you enter the grounds of Chesterholm you circumvent a boggy area that may be part of Vindo-landa's ancient rubbish dump. If so, it will eventually yield its treasures to the archaeologists.

The public footpath, for those not paying to visit Vindolanda, is clearly waymarked round the edge of the Chesterholm area, and emerges on the drive between the house and Stanegate.

To visit Vindolanda go to Chesterholm (where you can pay, and see the museum), then through the fort and the town, to come out onto the Stanegate by the large car-park.

Follow the Stanegate eastwards, back past the fort, which clearly dominates the old road. Drop down to the crossing of the burns at Codley Gate Farm, and the Roman milestone.

The lane leaves the line of the Stanegate and turns uphill, crossing the old Barcombe railway line and passing the small east car-park. It heads up to a T-junction on Barcombe.

❀ (If you have not climbed Barcombe, turn left up to the Crindledikes road junction, where a footpath goes up over the ridge (see pages 122-123)).

* For Bardon Mill via the Chineley Burn turn right at the T-junction and follow the lane for 250 metres. There are fine views over Vindolanda from the lane. A wall-stile starts a footpath that drops diagonally south-west down the hillside into the woods. You pick up the line of the old railway, which becomes more obvious beyond the remains of an old colliery. The footpath gradually diverges from the old track, on the lower side. At one point, high above the burn's gorge, it crosses a bare patch where a spoil-heap tipped down the hillside. This could be tricky if icy. The path continues through the woods and emerges at the road-junction at West-wood Cottages. Turn right down the hill, cross the burn, and pick up the outward route back to Bardon Mill

Bardon Mill and Vindolanda

● The Roman Milestone at Codley Gate is the only one in Britain still standing full-height (1.5 metres) in its original position. (There is another, broken, a mile west along the Stanegate)

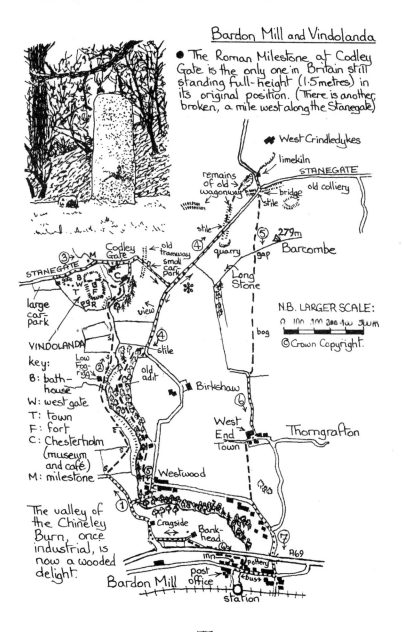

West Crindledykes

limekiln

STANEGATE

remains of old wagonway

old colliery

bridge

stile

stile

279m

STANEGATE

Codley Gate

old tramway

small car park

quarry

Barcombe

gap

Long Stone

3→ M

gate B W T F D R g R

large car park

VINDOLANDA

view

bog

N.B. LARGER SCALE:
0 100 2M 300 400 500 m
© Crown Copyright.

key:
B: bath-house
W: west gate
T: town
F: fort
C: Chesterholm (museum and café)
M: milestone

Low Fog-rigg

old adit

Birkshaw

West End Town

Thorngrafton

Westwood

The valley of the Chineley Burn, once industrial, is now a wooded delight.

Cragside

Bank-head

A69

inn

pottery

post office

bus

Bardon Mill

station

57

Beltingham

✳ From Bardon Mill cross the railway, then the Tyne by the long footbridge. Follow the lane eastwards, passing the riverside nature reserve, and go up onto the mound topped by Beltingham.

• Beltingham is about as "chocolate-box" as you will find along the Tyne. Its safe mound above the river meadows is topped by pretty cottages and the church of St. Cuthbert.

This is an old site of worship as attested by the remnant of the Saxon preaching cross by the East window (right). It is reputed to have been a brief resting point for the body of St. Cuthbert on its long travels to reach Durham. The church is delightful inside: the Perpendicular style fills it with light.

✳ Go down the bank before the vicarage into the wooded ravine. Follow the path up the other side, then across the edge of the fields towards Ridley Hall, which is hidden by the trees. Turn left down the lane to the junction, where keep right along the lane to the old walled garden.

● Allen Banks are a part of the estate of Ridley Hall. The latter is private, but the delightful wooded gorge and Morralee Wood are controlled by the National Trust.

This is a place to visit at any season — when ice and snow turn it into a winter wonderland, in the exuberance of spring and summer; in the rich colours of autumn.

● Plankey Mill, up the river Allen, is a popular summer venue. There camping and maybe refreshments can be found.

▲ <u>The Allen from Plankey Mill bridge.</u>

▼ <u>Plankey Mill suspension bridge</u>

59

<u>Allen Banks and Staward</u> : 14.5km or 5.5km (9 or 3¼ miles) of riverside, woods and pasture.

Start : at the National Trust carpark, in the old walled garden of Ridley Hall (signposted "Allen Banks").
Public transport : train and bus at Bardon Mill (2.7km); bus at Ridley Bridge (1km). infrequent bus at Staward Station (south end of walk).

✱ Consult the map-board, which shows many of the paths between here and Plankey Mill, then follow the riverside path south into the woods. In the first gorge you pass the short suspension bridge, without crossing. Go on upriver, out into the open below Plankey Mill, and back into woods to cross the footbridge over Kingswood Burn. The long suspension bridge to Plankey Mill is just beyond. Cross over. The path continues upstream on the east bank. Go through the camping field, over a stile and along the edge of a meadow (beautiful with flowers in late spring).
Enter the National Trust's Staward Gorge woodland. The path follows the twists of the gorge. As the valley broadens briefly the path divides. A steep path goes up through the conifer plantation onto a narrow ridge between the Allen gorge and deep Harsondale.......

● Suddenly across the ridge you encounter a massive, 3m high wall. This is the bastion of Staward Pele. Now there is not much to see amidst the trees. The wall blocking the ridge is all that remains of the great tower, and only one tall spur (right) remains of the gatehouse. But when the friars built it in the 14th century this must have been an impregnable stronghold, perched on the narrow ridge with a clear view in all directions (The woodland came much later: Staward Wood was planted in the 1790s).

✱ The path leaves the wood through a gate. You head up across the upland pasture onto the flat ridge towards the ruined cottage of Gingle Pot. A track goes on up to meet the road at Staward Station.......

● Staward Pele was a favourite picnic place for Victorians, who came to Staward Station on the erstwhile Allendale branch railway. Built in 1869 to serve the leadmining communities of Allendale, it was never a great success – it missed the villages it was supposed to serve, and the lead mines closed. The railway closed for passengers in 1930, and altogether in 1950.

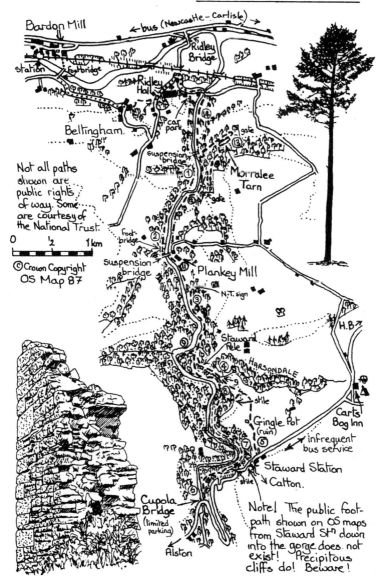

Bardon Mill

← bus (Newcastle – Carlisle) →

Ridley Bridge

station

footbridge

Ridley Hall

car park

Beltingham

gate

Not all paths shown are public rights of way. Some are courtesy of the National Trust.

suspension bridge

Morralee Tarn

gate

0   ½   1 km

© Crown Copyright OS Map 87

foot-bridge ②

suspension bridge

Plankey Mill

N.T. sign

H.B.

Staward Pele

④

HARSONDALE

stile

Gingle Pot (ruin)

Carts Bog Inn

infrequent bus service

Staward Station

↘ Calton.

stile

Cupola Bridge (limited parking)

↓ Alston

Note! The public foot-path shown on OS maps from Staward Stⁿ down into the gorge does not exist! Precipitous cliffs do! Beware!

Staward and Allen Banks : Staward Gorge.

✱ Leave Staward Station along the Alston road for 250 metres. A stile at the first bend offers a way down. The path is close to the wall above the wooded gorge. At the stile into the National Trust property you have a choice:

Turning right takes you along a high-level terrace through the woods, with fine views of the gorge. This is the official path north, suitable in any river conditions....

🐾 Turning left instead takes you on a descending path to Cupola Bridge.

Note larger scale:
0   500m
© Crown Copyright
Harsondale
Staward Pele
stile
stile
steps
Gingle Pot
riverbed route in fine weather
terrace
stile
Staward Station
N.T. sign
Cupola Bridge
(limited parking) (1778)

🐾 Downstream from Cupola Bridge a wild route hugs the riverbank round the first bend to a ruined lime-kiln. The path disappears. If the river is low you may wish to follow the shallows down the gorge. A well-placed sill provides a river-level route round the next curve. Climb up the lower bank beyond to regain the path.
Beware of flash flooding!

Gingle Pot.

* The high-level terrace path is carefully engineered across the steep slopes round the second bend of the river. Then it drops down to the level of the high riverside banks. (You may hear the sounds of wet walkers in the riverbed!). The path divides: the left-hand, riverside path is better.

This becomes an avenue of tall beech trees, along to a bend, then scrambles about somewhat, before abruptly diving through a screen of trees to rejoin the other path. This climbs again, and moves away from the river. It even climbs steps.

The path makes a T-junction with that coming down from Gingle Pot. (If you are coming the other way, the junction is surprisingly high in the wood.)

Turn left and follow the good path down, below the high-perched ruins of Staward Pele. The path returns you to river-level, and you can follow it all the way down to Plankey Mill....

Allen Banks and Staward : Morralee Wood.

✱ Leave Plankey Mill up the road. As it swings to the right keep straight on along a path. At first this is atop the mud bluffs, then it descends with the haughs to river level. After 500 metres of meadows the path and river enter the Allen gorge and the National Trust woodland. Again there is a choice of paths:

✻ To return quickly to the Allen Banks car park keep to the lower paths by the riverside, down to the suspension bridge or the road-bridge.

✱ Much more fun is to explore up into Morralee Wood: take paths upwards and to the right. Steps and terraces will take you up the cliffs of the gorge onto the plateau.

The path almost reaches a wicket gate at the south end of the wood, then heads back to the north amid the rhododendrons.

A complex net of paths meet at the high-point. North-eastwards and downwards should take you down to the tarn. Enjoy its peace and quiet.

From its east end two tracks go down eastwards. That on the right leads to a gate and a field-path to a road. You want the left-hand path, that soon turns back on itself and contours through the beautiful woodland.

At a crossing of paths keep straight on. You will probably feel that you are walking in circles! The path goes down to the suspension bridge. Either cross over and follow the riverside path down to the car-park or keep to the east bank down to the roadbridge. Then the car-park is just along to the left.

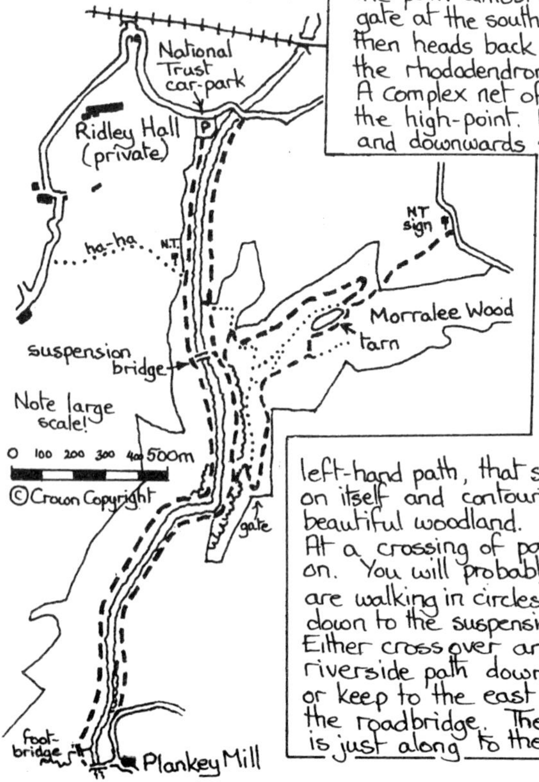

National Trust car-park

Ridley Hall (private)

ha-ha. N.T.

N.T. sign

Morralee Wood tarn

suspension bridge

Note large scale!

0 100 200 300 400 500m

© Crown Copyright

gate

foot-bridge

Plankey Mill

● Morralee Wood and Tarn are part of the National Trust's Allen Banks property. They used to be in the grounds of Ridley Hall. The carefully engineered paths, and the woodland itself are products of the feudal system and of the growing appreciation of woodland and parkland scenery in the late 18th century.

Bardon Mill to Haydon Bridge (9.0 km, 5½ miles)

✱ From Bardon Mill go down the lane and over the level crossing. The long footbridge takes you over the South Tyne. Turn left along the lane to Beltingham, passing the Nature Reserve. Go on up into Beltingham (see previous pages). Beside the vicarage go down the bank into the Beltingham Burn ravine. Follow the footpath up the other side and across the field edges towards Ridley Hall. Turn left down the lane to the Hall gate, where you bear right along the lane to Allen Banks car-park (National Trust). (There are toilets here).

  There are paths up both banks of the River Allen. Use either to reach the suspension bridge......

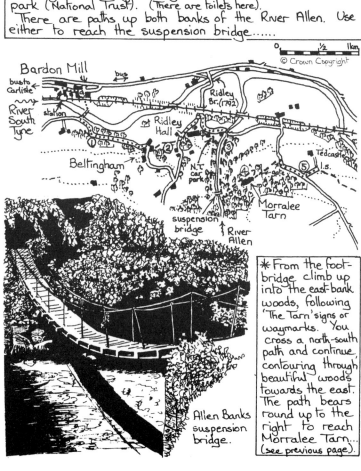

0   ½   1km

© Crown Copyright

Bardon Mill

bus to Carlisle ←

bus →

Ridley Br. (1792)

River South Tyne

station

Ridley Hall

Beltingham

① ② ③ ④ ⑤

Tedcastle l.s.

N.T. car park

gate

Morralee Tarn

suspension bridge

↑ River Allen

Allen Banks suspension bridge.

✱ From the foot-bridge climb up into the east-bank woods, following 'The Tarn' signs or waymarks. You cross a north-south path and continue contouring through beautiful woods towards the east. The path bears round up to the right to reach Morralee Tarn...
(see previous page).

66

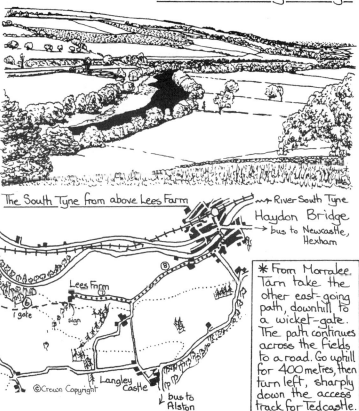

The South Tyne from above Lees Farm

River South Tyne

Haydon Bridge
→ bus to Newcastle, Hexham

Lees Farm ⑦

⑥ gate

sign

⑧

©Crown Copyright

Langley Castle

↓ bus to Alston

*From Morralee. Tarn take the other east-going path, downhill to a wicket-gate. The path continues across the fields to a road. Go uphill for 400 metres, then turn left, sharply down the access track for Tedcastle.

At the sharp left bend a ladder-stile invites you into the fields. From here there is a discrepancy between the right-of-way and the actual path on the ground. The r-o-w heads diagonally and pathlessly up the bank to an unseen ladder-stile. The clear field-path rejoins it at a plank bridge over a ditch. Together they head for the top of the wood, where the gateway offers a suddenly-different view down the Tyne Valley.

Lees Farm is your next objective: the path goes down the hillside, keeping a wall on the left, to the south-west corner of the farmyard (signpost). Go through the yard, and follow the farm track and then the lane down into Haydon Bridge.

Haydon Bridge

● <u>Haydon Bridge</u>, as its name implies, is an ancient bridging point over the South Tyne. There was a bridge here at the start of the 14th century, and in 1323 a charter was granted for a market. The bridge had to be rebuilt after the great Tyne Flood of 1773, and in 1806 the collapse of one arch required the rebuild of three. As traffic developed the bridge became a bottleneck as traffic queued to cross its narrow spans. This was relieved by the building of the <u>new concrete road-bridge</u>, so that traffic can roar through unhindered.

- The town itself has moved. In mediæval times it stood up on the hillside, clear of the river. Now little remains of Old Haydon except the <u>old church of St. Cuthbert</u>. A church has been in existence here since at least the ninth century, and the building itself contains late Norman parts. The font is a re-used Roman altar! The church was abandoned in 1795, and slighted, when the <u>new St. Cuthbert's</u> opened in the growing township down the hill. But it was restored in 1882 using original stonework where possible, and sits quietly up on the hillside amid the yews.
- Haydon Bridge has been a seat of learning in the valley ever since the grammar school was set up by bequest in 1685.

- The town also boasts a proper share of facilities:

—4 inns/hotels
—4 churches (CoE, RC, URC, Meths)
— a post-office
— a bank
— shops
— a "chippy"
— a station (with a sparse but useful train service).
— buses along the valley.
What more do you want?

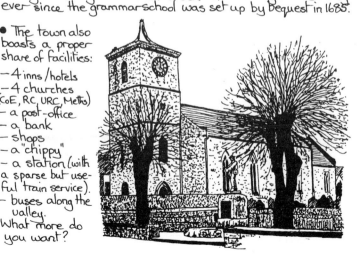

Haydon Bridge and Langley Castle (circular).   8.6 km

* Cross the Bridge to the south bank and turn right. Along at the corner turn up left in front of the Shaftoe School, — the original Haydon Bridge school dating from 1685. Go up round the school onto a back lane, above the houses. Follow this along, and continue on the footpath that dips down suddenly to a footbridge over the burn in Gee's Wood. Follow one of the paths upstream through the delightful little wood, emerging too soon onto the Alston road. Follow it 400 metres downhill to its junction with the valley road. There a stile and sign point a way south-eastwards across the fields through a string of gates to a stile into the wood. A footbridge takes you over Crossley Burn, and an old ponytrack continues up through charming Elrington Wood. A stile shows the way onwards as a field-path, south towards Elrington. Before reaching the farm turn hard right, past a lodge, and follow the track round the hillside to the bridge over the Elrington Burn. Go through the gate on the bridge, then bear right through another 70 metres along. This track winds delightfully through the woods to Threepwood. It continues gently uphill to the south-west, becoming a tractor-track. It clings to one side of a wall and then the other along the hillside towards Langley Castle, with extensive views. The path drops down into the woods opposite the castle, and after twists and turns emerges onto the Alston road, just outside the Castle entrance drive.

(5½ miles) of woodland, farm-land and lanes.

Haydon Bridge and Langley Castle

Haydon Bridge
Footbridge
101m
East Land Ends
wool
West Land Ends
wool
150m
Threepwood
lane
woo5m
DinneHey
Elrington
Castle Fm
Langley Castle
0   ½   1km
© Crown Copyright
O.S. Map 87.

● Langley Castle, now a restaurant and banqueting hall, was built in the fourteenth century as a substantial tower house. It is every little boy's idea of a castle, with a strong tower on each corner, four-square. It changed hands between Northumberland families until acquired by the Radcliffes in 1632. After their disaster in the 1715 uprising the Crown confiscated the Castle and gave it to the Greenwich Hospital. It was bought and restored in the 1890s by the antiquarian Cadwallader Bates. Since then it has been a school, and now a restaurant.

* At the sharp bend just below Langley Castle a lane branches west to Castle Farm, where a green lane heads straight down the hillside towards the river. At West Land Ends a lane takes you directly down into Haydon Bridge.

✳ As there is no continuous riverside path downstream from Haydon Bridge, take to the hillside for a change of scene. Cross the level crossing by the station. A little way up the hill a driveway goes to the Roman Catholic church. A ladder stile starts a path that climbs the grassy hillside to Tofts.

To visit Haydon Old Church, walk east along the lane. The views over the valley are excellent. Return the same way.

Now there is a kilometre of road, climbing up past Cruelsike across Haydon Fell. The views west, and north-west towards the Wall country, develop as you gain height.

At the crossroads escape into the rough pasture. Head north-east towards the far corner. Two wall-stiles give onto the uninspiring top of Haydon Fell. Sheep tracks take you down past the plantation, with views east. Beyond 2 gates the tracks become indistinct over rough pasture. Go up to a wall along the ridge (this seems to have a stile missing, in 1992). From the wall you can see the direction down to Settlingstones Farm, where you meet the Stanegate.....

● The Stanegate is one of the oldest parts of the Romans' defensive system, predating the famous Wall by twenty years or so. A good road, with forts every seven miles was the key to defence against the wild men of the north. One of the forts was at Newbrough, where St. Peter's Church sits in its centre!

✳ Follow the Stanegate downhill to the east for 1½ km. A gate beyond the second set of cottages opens onto a footpath down the hillside to a footbridge at Stonecroft. Go on down the lane to rejoin the Stanegate, and go along to St. Peter's....

72

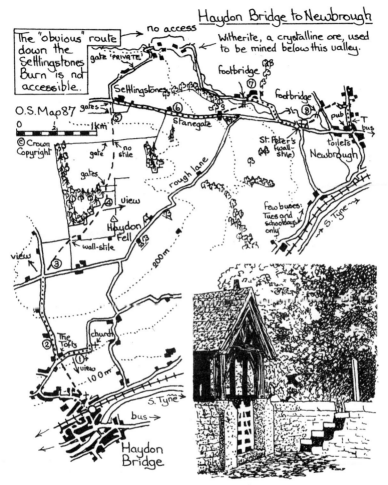

no access

Witherite, a crystalline ore, used to be mined below this valley.

The "obvious" route down the Settlingstones Burn is not accessible.

gate 'PRIVATE'

footbridge ⑦

footbridge

Settlingstones

⑥

O.S. Map 87

gates

⑤

Stanegate

pub

bus

© Crown Copyright

0   1km

gate

no stile

rough lane

St Peter's (wall-stile)

⑧

toilets

Newbrough

gates

④ view

Haydon Fell

200 m

Few buses Tues and schooldays only

S. Tyne

view

③

wall-stile

The Tofts

②

church

① view

100 m

S. Tyne

bus →

Haydon Bridge

● St Peter's Church was built in 1865, when Newbrough was enjoying the prosperity from its coal mine, ore mine and quarry. Its stands on the site of a 1242 chapel, in a Roman fort.

* A wall-stile leads into the churchyard. A gate leads to a path down to another footbridge. Climb the far side, cross a track, and wiggle through to meet the drive from Newbrough Hall. Newbrough, with the Red Lion, is just down the hill.

Newbrough to West Boat. (5.2 km, 3.4 miles one way).

• Newbrough, predictably, is not 'new'. The "new burh" dates back to the early 13th century: Henry III granted a charter for a market. During its mining prosperity in the 19th century the village even acquired a town hall! Now it has the pub, church and a bus service to Hexham.

✱ Go south down the quiet lane opposite the Red Lion. Down on the right the Settlingstones Burn makes its way to the river. Turn right, briefly, at the main road, then almost immediately left to a house standing beside the railway. The path goes down next to the embankment to pass under the tracks next to the burn.

Now the path follows the riverbank eastwards, with the railway as close company as far as Fourstones. Well beyond the village the path cuts a corner as the river forms a sharp bend.

Note Warden Hill, up on your left. This stands in the fork of the Tynes, and is visited on a later page.

The riverside path emerges from the bushes next to the paper-mill and level crossing — a suddenly industrial scene. Follow the road along to West Boat.

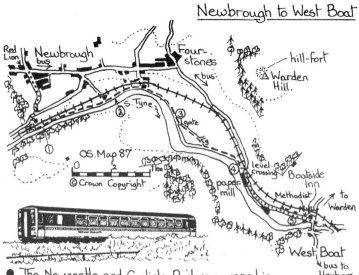

● The Newcastle and Carlisle Railway opened in stages between 1835 and 1839, and helped the spread of industry and prosperity along the Tyne Valley. Every little place had its sidings and little branches, such as the paper-mill at Warden and the quarries around Fourstones. Now these sidings — and the station at Fourstones — have gone. The heavy freight trains now connect other parts, using the only cross-country line between Edinburgh and Leeds.

The South Tyne below Fourstones.

Warden

● Warden is a quiet little village in the fork of the Tynes. Warden Hill, above, would have been an important look-out point, with its views up both valleys.

● Warden Church was established in 704 AD. The building dates back to the eleventh century in parts, especially the tower base. (The top section was added in 1765: warning fires lit on the roof had caused appreciable damage!). The archway from the nave into the tower incorporates Roman stonework, presumably from Chesters.

● In 635 AD Oswald, the Christian king of Northumbria, won a decisive battle over the pagan Welsh (under Cadwalla), at the Battle of Heavenfield, just 4km north-east of Warden. After the battle preaching crosses were set up in the kingdom, as centres for public worship. Warden Cross, standing outside the church in the corner between tower and porch is one such, re-erected here in 1957.

- The church interior is mainly Victorian Gothic, following a rebuild of the chancel in the late 19th century, and the nave in 1765. But there are 13th century elements, particularly in the transepts (eg the lancet and double-lancet windows).

- The <u>font</u> looks very modern in its austere simplicity, that so well complements the 11th century archway behind it. Actually it dates from 1868, during the Gothic restoration. Wonders never cease!

- In the porch and church are several interesting coffins and grave-covers. One is the "Warden Man", which has been variously thought to be a reworked Roman altar piece, or 12th century.

- The ornately-carved <u>lych-gate</u> at the entrance to the graveyard dates back to 1903.

Note too the mounting block:

✱ From Warden walk down the lane to West Boat, passing under the Newcastle-Carlisle railway. Cross the Bridge and turn left just beyond. Just past the first houses look for the start of the riverbank path. It is not obvious. It starts beside a house drive, and dives into the bushes behind the other house gardens. Follow the path downstream, under the railway bridge (seen _above_ from Warden Bridge), and go past the piers of an earlier rail bridge. Just beyond you reach the <u>confluence of the Tynes</u>. (below). It is remarkably <u>un</u>spectacular, especially in summer when it can be shallow enough to wade across – but don't! ....

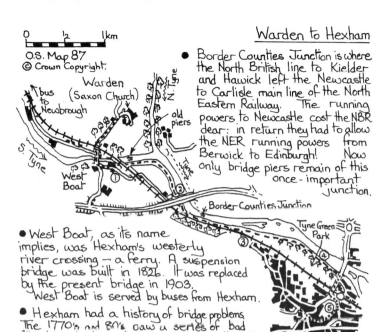

O.S. Map 87
© Crown Copyright.

Warden
(Saxon Church)

bus to Newbrough

Tyne

old piers

S. Tyne

West Boat

Border Counties Junction

Tyne Green Park

HEXHAM

● Border Counties Junction is where the North British line to Kielder and Hawick left the Newcastle to Carlisle main line of the North Eastern Railway. The running powers to Newcastle cost the NBR dear: in return they had to allow the NER running powers from Berwick to Edinburgh! Now only bridge piers remain of this once-important junction.

● West Boat, as its name implies, was Hexham's westerly river crossing — a ferry. A suspension bridge was built in 1826. It was replaced by the present bridge in 1903. West Boat is served by buses from Hexham.

● Hexham had a history of bridge problems. The 1770's and 80's saw a series of bad floods, which washed away three attempts at building Hexham Bridge. The present Hexham Bridge (Nº4) dates from 1793.

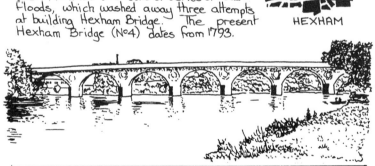

* (continued). From the Tyne confluence go on downriver, and pass under the A69 bridge. The path continues between river and railway past Border Counties Junction to reach Tyne Green Park. A lovely avenue of trees takes you towards Hexham Bridge. Along here, on sunny afternoons, you will find people really appreciating this open space.
Go round past the station, glimpsing Hexham's industrial side, and climb the long curving footpath, past the massive carpark, up towards the Abbey.

Chapter Three: the Roman Wall.

This chapter involves a new start, whether you have completed Chapter One, or one and Two, or are just starting. Brampton is easily reached by bus (and nearly reached by train) from either Haltwhistle or Hexham.

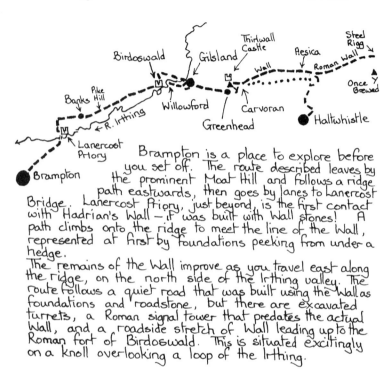

Brampton is a place to explore before you set off. The route described leaves by the prominent Moat Hill and follows a ridge path eastwards, then goes by lanes to Lanercost Bridge. Lanercost Priory, just beyond, is the first contact with Hadrian's Wall — it was built with Wall stones! A path climbs onto the ridge to meet the line of the Wall, represented at first by foundations peeking from under a hedge.

The remains of the Wall improve as you travel east along the ridge, on the north side of the Irthing valley. The route follows a quiet road that was built using the Wall as foundations and roadstone, but there are excavated turrets, a Roman signal tower that predates the actual Wall, and a roadside stretch of Wall leading up to the Roman fort of Birdoswald. This is situated excitingly on a knoll overlooking a loop of the Irthing.

Lanercost Priory

Brampton to Hexham

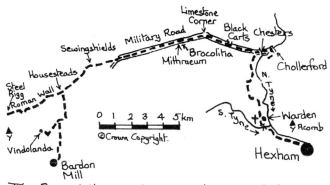

The River Irthing cuts across the Wall at Birdoswald. To visit the impressive Roman bridge remains at Willow-ford needs a detour through Gilsland. A superb section of excavated Wall stretches east from the river, complete with turrets, and a milecastle perched precariously on the County boundary.

From Gilsland to Greenhead you follow field-paths along the line of the Wall, but with little stonework on view. Near Greenhead you join the Pennine Way and pass ruined Thirlwall Castle. The route strides east along the Nine Nicks of Thirlwall, and on along the Whinstone ridge, in company with superb stretches of excavated Wall. En route you pass remains of Roman forts at Carvoran, Great Chesters and Housesteads. There are turrets and milecastles, Broad Wall and Narrow Wall, crags and loughs: this is splendid walking by anybody's standards.

A link route to or from Haltwhistle, by the delightful burn, is described. So too is a link from Housesteads to Vindolanda — a Roman fort and town — and Bardon Mill. The latter may be used by those who want to avoid the walk along Wade's Military Road, that adopts the line of the Wall east of Sewingshields all the way to Chesters. For those who stick with the Wall despite the road there are the attractions of the Temple to Mithras at Brocolitia, and the Roman fort and museum at Chesters. A detour to visit the bridge remains is suggested.

A walk along quiet lanes, and footpaths over Warden Hill brings you to lovely Warden church, and a river-side walk takes you on into Hexham.

Brampton

● The Moot Hall (1817) is at the east end of the market place. The upstairs meeting room is octagonal. Below nestles the tourist information centre.

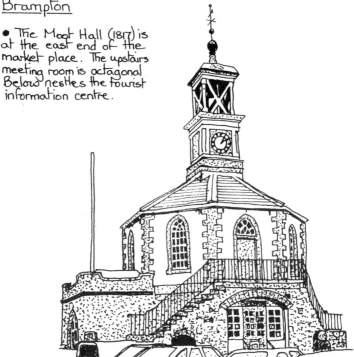

● Situated in the Borderlands, near Liddesdale and the Debatable Lands, where the writ of kings was ignored more than observed, where border-raiding and rustling was a way of life, Brampton might be expected to nestle securely within massive town walls. But no: not a wall in sight, nor even a tower or bastle. There had been a castle, an early motte-and-bailey on the Moat Hill at the east end of the town (right), but it had not been rebuilt in stone. The local castle, Naworth, home of the Warden of the West March, was several miles away, and afforded the town little direct protection. So how did Brampton survive the turbulent 16th century? Did this little town adopt an open-town policy rather than suffer repeated sieges and their aftermath, or was it too poverty-stricken to matter?

• Nowadays Brampton is still open to visitors, and offers small-market-town facilities: banking; shops; fish-and-chips; cafés; accommodation; hotels; an information office (seasonal). Buses link Brampton with Carlisle and the Tyne Valley — Greenhead, Haltwhistle, Bardon Mill, Hexham and Newcastle. In summer infrequent buses may run to Lanercost, Birdoswald, and Gilsland. The railway station is 3km away.

Moat Hill.

* Towards the east end of town a signpost points up onto the 'Moat Hill', site of the old motte castle. Make your way up to the top, crossing the ramparts. The view back over the town is superb.

Turn round and head away from the town, descending to meet the top of an access drive, then continuing north east along the Ridge Walk. A line of beeches is on your right. Enjoy the views to the north, across the Debatable Lands, the forgotten quarter of Cumberland. At a gate, enter the wood, courtesy of the Woodland Trust, and continue along a delightful avenue. Beyond another gate bear left along the top edge of the conifer wood, then follow the path down diagonally under the dark canopy. From a gate at the bottom corner of the wood go along level to meet a minor road. Turn left, briefly, then right, continuing north-east along the quiet lane. It soon joins a busier lane, downhill towards Lanercost Mill and Bridge.....

• Lanercost Bridge is an elegant, if narrow, two-arch Tudor bridge. Too frail and tight for modern traffic, it is paralleled by a concrete structure opened in 1962.

* The footpath goes upriver beside the Irthing for about 400m (¼mile), then turns abruptly towards the east side of the Priory.

Brampton to Lanercost

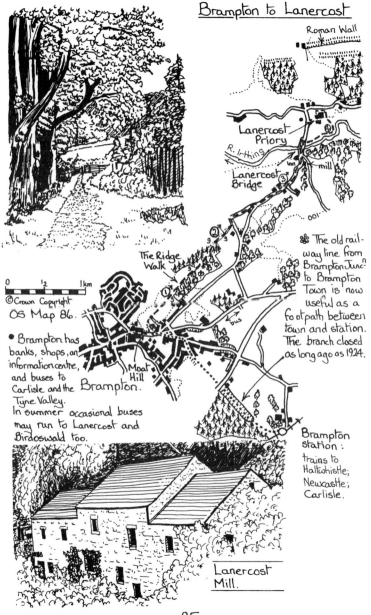

Roman Wall

Lanercost
Priory

R. Irthing

Lanercost
Bridge

The Ridge
Walk

0   ½   1km

© Crown Copyright
OS Map 86.

• Brampton has
banks, shops, an
information centre,
and buses to
Carlisle and the
Tyne Valley.
In summer occasional buses
may run to Lanercost and
Birdoswald too.

Moat
Hill

Brampton.

❀ The old rail-
way line from
Brampton Junc.ⁿ
to Brampton
Town is now
useful as a
footpath between
town and station.
The branch closed
as long ago as 1924.

Brampton
station:
trains to
Haltwhistle;
Newcastle;
Carlisle.

Lanercost
Mill.

85

Lanercost Priory

- The priory was founded in 1166 as a Priory of Augustinian Canons. Its setting, by the River Irthing was — and is — beautiful, and no doubt suited its Norman founder, Robert de Vaux, lord of Gilsland. But here on the border between the emerging nations of England and Scotland it was doomed to a far from peaceful existence. The not long completed priory was attacked by Scots in 1296 and 1297, and was then used as a personal base by Edward I in three of his campaigns against Scotland. Indeed, from September 1306 to March 1307 Lanercost was the seat of English government. Edward was ill, and took time to partially recover at Lanercost before calling a Parliament in Carlisle. After Edward's death the Scots returned, in the person of Robert Bruce, to wreak vengeance on the canons, in 1311.

The border tensions of the 16th century did not stop Henry VIII including Lanercost in his first round of ecclesiastical privatisations in 1536. The canons were dispersed, and the roof and other valuables removed.

Lanercost Priory gatehouse.

Lanercost Priory.

The south-east corner.

- After the Dissolution a small section of the north aisle of the church was left usable as the parish church. In the 18th century this was extended, with the nave reroofed and walled off from the rest of the ruins. The church continues in active use.

- The priory ruins — the chancel and transepts of the old church, plus the priory buildings, are in the care of English Heritage. They may be visited, for a small fee, in the summer months.
The ruins and church are built with a mixture of sandstone blocks, much of it the beautiful deep red local stone. The source for much of this dressed stone is not hard to find — it comes from Hadrian's Wall, just a kilometre to the north! Some stones with Roman inscriptions can be seen.

- The Lanercost Cross dates from 1214. The base sits on the green north of the church. It appears to have been much used for sword-sharpening! The head, after a period in use in the graveyard, now resides in the north-west corner of the nave.

Lanercost Priory to Birdoswald.

8.5 km (5¼ miles), mainly quiet roads, but interesting.

● Pike Hill signal tower is older than Hadrian's Wall. It is set at an angle to the later Wall, but has been deeply cut into by the road.

0 ½ 1km
© Crown Copyright

△ 177m

Wall bowers

150 — turret 51A →   ⑤

turret 51B →   ④

rebuilt Wall

Turret 52A   car park

Hare Hill   ②   ③ signal tower

Haytongate   ①

Banks

River Irthing

Lanercost Priory

Low Row

bus

Abbey Inn

● Banks East Turret, 52A, is the first significant Wall ruin met

• Hadrian's Wall is met for the first time in this section. This western section was originally built of turf, with stone turrets, but was later converted to stone to match the rest. The Turf Wall was on a different line just west of Birdoswald.

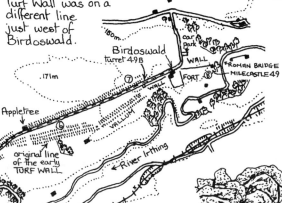

• The 3 metre high fragment of Wall at Hare Hill is impressive (below). But it is a Victorian reconstruction on original foundations.

* Leave Lanercost by the old gate-house, turning right up the lane to the crossroads. Go straight on, and wind up the farm track to Haytongate.
There you head east, on the south side of the hedge that rises from the foundations of Hadrian's Wall. This is visible in places.
At Hare Hill you wind down the corkscrew farm drive, pausing at the rebuilt Wall section. Go on down to the lane, go a few metres left, then right up the hill to Banks.
Follow the lane east along the ridge. Fragments of Hadrian's Wall begin to appear in stone. The ditch keeps you company all the way to Birdoswald.

Birdoswald.

- <u>Birdoswald Turret</u>, 49B, to the west of Birdoswald on the Stone Wall. The original Wall, between Willowford Bridge and the Solway, was constructed in turf, with stone turrets at intervals. Turf was a familiar material for the Roman army — it was used for their normal route camps. But in time the turfs did shrink (this can be seen with the replica wall sections at Vindolanda). At some stage it was decided to replace the Turf Wall with stone. Mostly the rebuilt Wall followed the original line, but at Birdoswald a new line was chosen for a few miles. The original Wall met the fort in the usual position, south of the main east and west gates. The new Wall butted on to the corners of the fort.

As elsewhere, the Wall was robbed for building stone, then used as a superb foundation for a road.

new stone Wall

new stone Wall

new turret 49B

←west gate

==== original Turf Wall

↑ tower

east gate

= ==== Turf Wall

granaries (excavated)

south gate

NOT TO SCALE.

↙ view

Site of Iron Age fort.

- **Birdoswald** is impressive, even as you approach. A solid section of Hadrian's Wall provides an introduction whether you come from east or west, and is reflected in the solid walls of the fort itself, with the farm-buildings tucked into the north-west corner. A tower stands tall and martial, overlooking the whole. The fort is in the care of Cumbria County Council, and is in process of excavation. A visitor centre welcomes you during the summer months, and provides refreshments as well as information. Detailed guides to the fort and its surroundings are available. A fee is payable to visit the fort (reduced for English Heritage members). An infrequent bus service may run during the summer, connecting to Brampton, Lanercost Priory, Gilsland, Greenhead, Aesica and Haltwhistle.

- The **tower** forms part of the farm-house. Despite its looks it is not a mediaeval peel tower, but a Victorian romantic addition! The farm-house dates from the 16th century, with later additions, rebuilds and modifications.

- The **fort** is enormous. Only part has been excavated, but the granaries, with great doorways, stone floors and buttressed walls, are most impressive. Do not neglect the southern end, up the slope – it is worth the effort.

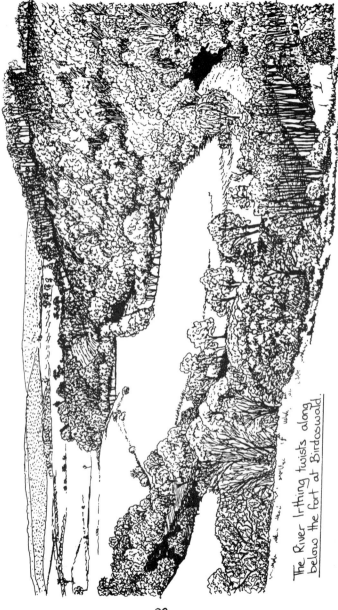

The River Irthing twists along below the fort at Birdoswald.

Birdoswald.

- Unsuspected from the road, or even from the visitors' centre or the granaries at the north end of the fort, is the dramatic drop to the River Irthing. Do visit the south end of the fort and pass through the south gateway. Suddenly you will see why the fort is built just here. A promontory juts southwards, 60 metres (200 feet) above the river twisting below. An Iron Age fort occupied this aerie before the Romans. Southwards the land rises in waves towards the Pennine skyline.

- Harrow Scar milecastle (No 49) also occupies a strategic point above a bend in the river, a half-kilo-metre to the east. Leave Birdoswald fort past the impressive dual carriageway east gate (above), and accompany a solid section of Wall to the milecastle (below). A popular pastime along this wall is to hunt for the many Roman inscriptions — but there are hundreds of thousands of stones to look on!
The milecastle overlooks the site of the Willowford Roman Bridge, and the continuing Wall. But the voracious river has eaten away the tall bank and the bridge. Most walkers will have to journey through Gilsland to reach the far bank.

93

Birdoswald to Willowford. 3.5km (2¼ miles) of lanes, paths and an excellent stretch of Roman Wall.

This section is complicated enormously by the River Irthing: the Roman Wall crossed the river by a bridge just below milecastle 49 (Harrow Scar). But the river has shifted, the bridge has gone and the bank has been cut steeper. The river may be forded in favourable conditions, but most walkers will choose to walk round via Gilsland:

＊ Having visited Harrow Scar milecastle, return along the Wall to the fort. Go north down the lane to beyond the carpark. Two ladder-stiles show where a field-path begins, and where it drops over the valley side. A footbridge carries the path over Harrow's Beck. The path disappears crossing the boggy fields towards The Hill. A stile gives access to the lane, which you follow downhill to Gilsland.

Cross the River Irthing on the substantial road-bridge, then turn right up the hill. You meet the line of the Wall again by the erstwhile vicarage on the top of the hill. On the right a notice-board stands proudly next to a substantial stretch of Wall.

Follow the farm-track along beside the Wall. Turret 48A has been excavated. Parts of the Wall have been carried away by the bank erosion of the Irthing, visible far below.

The farm-track crosses the Wall, but you continue on its south side over a switchback, to reach turret 48B and the farm of Willowford.

At the farm pay a small fee for the privilege of visiting the bridge, then descend the bank, on the north side of the Wall, to the Roman Bridge abutment.

Turret 48A : note the step in the Wall gauge.

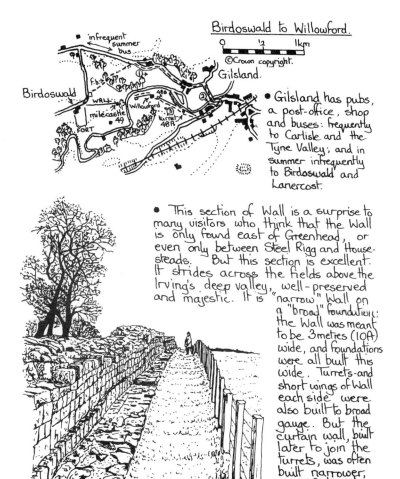

Birdoswald to Willowford.

0   ½   1km

©Crown copyright.

Gilsland.

• Gilsland has pubs, a post-office, shop and buses: frequently to Carlisle and the Tyne Valley; and in summer infrequently to Birdoswald and Lanercost.

• This section of Wall is a surprise to many visitors who think that the Wall is only found east of Greenhead, or even only between Steel Rigg and House-steads. But this section is excellent. It strides across the fields above the Irving's deep valley, well-preserved and majestic. It is "narrow" Wall on a "broad" foundation: the Wall was meant to be 3 metres (10ft) wide, and foundations were all built this wide. Turrets - and short wings of Wall each side were also built to broad gauge. But the curtain wall, built later to join the turrets, was often built narrower, just 8 feet wide. (Presumably an economy drive caught up with the original plans!)

The ragged foot left on the South face of the Wall can be clearly seen, as above, where the Wall swoops over the slopes east of Willowford.

Willowford

● The Roman Bridge abutment, and the Wall rising up to Willowford Farm, seen from across the river at Harrow Scar.

● The Romans were thorough about their Wall. A river cutting across it was no excuse for a gap. So here, as at Chesters, there was a bridge to complete the Wall. This originally linked the stone-built Wall east of the Irthing, with the Turf Wall built on the west bank. The abutment on the east bank incorporates water channels that may have been related to a mill, or for flood water. The bridge was rebuilt twice, and enlarged. A great masonry block was built to help protect the upstream side, and the bridge was widened to carry the Military Road.

Willowford.

• The <u>bridge abutment</u> at Willowford. The two original water channels are on the left, one of them blocked by rebuilding. The larger channel on the right is part of later work. Information boards on site give a clear indication of the various stages of construction and rebuilding. Nothing remains of the other piers, the western abutment or the Wall (either turf or stone) up to Harrow Scar milecastle. The river has ground its course further down the underlying slope over the years, cutting away the opposite hillside in the process.

• <u>East of Willowford Farm.</u>

• <u>Poltross Burn</u> forms the boundary between Cumberland and Northumberland. There is found milecastle 48, clinging perilously to the steep slope. Considering how close it is to the town, it is a wonder that any of it survives, but it is in remarkable condition. It has been excavated, and the walls of the barrack rooms can be traced easily. Did the beds (bunks?) that the garrison used have odd length legs (like haggis), or did the troops roll downhill to wake in a sordid heap each morning? The footpath descends steeply to a footbridge over the burn, next to the tall railway bridge.

• <u>Across the fields past Gap</u> the Ditch is very prominent. This fighting ditch fronted the Wall wherever there were no crags, and meant that attackers had to struggle uphill to approach the Wall. It provided an effective tank-trap to deter use of siege engines or battering rams by the more literate of their enemies!
Ahead, the Nine Nicks of Thirlwall serrate the skyline.

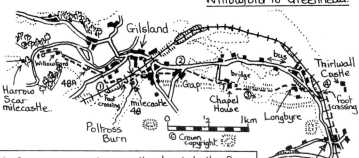

* Retrace your steps up the bank to the farm at Willowford, and along beside the Wall and turrets to the Gilsland road. Cross over, and negotiate a boggy way round the west side of the house there. A path climbs up to a foot-crossing over the Newcastle-Carlisle railway. Watch out for trains! A short way along beside the line you reach Poltross Burn mile-castle, clinging to the slope above the burn.

Greenhead. (pub, youth hostel, buses..).

Cross the burn into Northumberland, and follow the footpath along to the subway under the railway. If you want stores (or anything else) in Gilsland, go under and down the bank. Otherwise, turn up right to regain the line of the Wall, along to a road. A ladder-stile, just downhill, indicates the way onwards across the fields, following the Ditch embankments, to Gap. Go through the farmyard and down the lane briefly. From another stile the path rises gently across fields, up to a stile high beside the line of the Wall, then descends to meet the track to Chapel House.

Go between the buildings, cross a little footbridge where a burn runs along the Ditch, and continue eastwards. The earthworks of the Wall are very obvious here, stretching towards Thirlwall Castle in the distance. The line of Ditch and Wall climbing the hillside towards Carvoran is also very obvious, and the Nine Nicks of Thirlwall punctuate the sky-line ahead.

The path dips to cross another rivulet before reaching Long-byre. Keep to the south side of the Wall along to the main road. There is an excavated section of Wall in the road cutting. Walk south along the road to the cottages (where there are bus-stops for the desperate!). Cross the railway-another foot-crossing — and turn right along a footpath between the railway and the Tipalt Burn, into Greenhead.

99

✱ The lane past the youth hostel in Greenhead, on the east side of the railway, becomes a footpath squeezed between the line and the burn. Continue to a stile, where the Pennine Way crosses the tracks. Do not cross, but follow the P.W. east, over the small burn and alongside the larger Tipalt Burn to Thirlwall Castle. Cross the Tipalt Burn by the footbridge by the cottages below the castle. A walled lane zigzags uphill into a belt of trees. The Way continues uphill on the north side of the fighting ditch of the Roman Wall. Even after 1600 years of neglect the potency of the defensive ditch is still evident.
At the lane turn right to the crossroads at Carvoran.

• Thirlwall Castle is a fourteenth century tower, built with stone from the Roman Wall between here and Carvoran. This gap in the hills was an obvious route for the Scots, and several castles were raised along the valley for protection. It was occupied until the 18th century. Since then it has decayed — or in its turn been quarried to build or repair the cottages. Even since Wainwright recorded it in his "Pennine Way Companion" (1967) it has suffered significant collapse.

Greenhead to Carvoran

Thirlwall Castle

ditch

Walltown Quarry

foot crossing

stile

Youth Hostel

bus stops

Greenhead (hotel; Y.H.; post office; church; buses to Brampton, Carlisle, Hexham and Newcastle).

Carvoran (museum)

MAGNIS (Roman Fort)

©Crown Copyright

❀ Alternative: Climb out of Greenhead up the B6318, up to the bend. A gate lets you into a field. Aim up to the right, where a wall-stile shows the way to the hilltop and the remains of the Roman fort, MAGNIS, and Carvoran.

● The house contains a Roman Army Museum. This has displays to illustrate garrison life on the Wall. There is also a coffee-shop (within the museum. There is an entry fee. Buses may reach here in summer.

● Carvoran is older than Hadrian's Wall. Commanding the strategic gap between Tyne and Irthing, it lies at the junction of the Stanegate and the Maiden Way (from Lancashire via Cross Fell) There is little to see of the fort itself - it was levelled by the farmer in 1837 to prevent sightseeing! The north-west tower still protrudes through the turf, and its superb position is apparent as you look down at the web of transport routes through Greenhead.

Carvoran to Great Chesters 4.7km (3 miles).

✱ From the Carvoran crossroads a lane runs east, with a path alongside, past Walltown West Quarry. Beyond the cattlegrid strike back uphill to the crest of the ridge, by the rim of the quarry. Follow the excellent section of Roman Wall eastwards, up and down over the Nine Nicks of Thirlwall to reach Turret 45A.

Drop downhill and skirt the edge of Walltown East Quarry to rejoin the roller-coaster ridge. Follow the unexcavated Wall along to Walltown Gap. Descend carefully and cross the gap, passing King Arthur's Well. (Here Paulinus is said to have baptised one of the kings of Northumbria).

Climb steeply uphill to Turret 44B, and stop to admire the view......

• Walltown Quarry was established to exploit the Whin Sill. This ridge of exceedingly hard basaltic rock was left standing proud of the softer surrounding rocks by the grinding of the Ice Age. The Romans built their Wall on the jagged remnants, but used sandstone for the Wall itself; the basalt was too hard for them to use for building. Later technology allowed its quarrying by blasting and mechanical crushing. The huge quarries produced thousands of tons of roadstone before they closed in 1978. Now there are plans to refill the western quarry partially, and even to build a full-height replica section of Wall, complete with turrets!

Walltown East Quarry

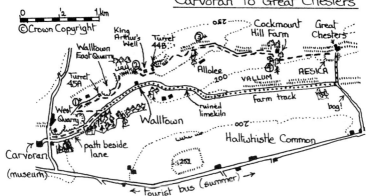

• <u>Hadrian's Wall between the quarries</u> was excavated in 1958 and stands proudly up to nine courses high. As it follows the undulating terrain you can see how the courses run parallel to gentle slopes, but become stepped on steeper ground. Turret 45A, overlooking the east quarry, appears to have been built earlier than the other Wall turrets: usually turrets were built with short wings of Wall on each side, to aid attachment of the in-between Wall when it was added. But here the Wall butts roughly up to the turret itself, which is at a slight angle too. Perhaps it was an early lookout tower. Certainly it commands an excellent view!

> ❀ The lane past Walltown provides a less exciting but less exposed alternative route. It gives an excellent closeup view of the Vallum.

Turret 44B, overlooking Walltown

● The Walltown, now an isolated farmhouse, is in Ridley country. Here lived John Ridley, cousin to Bishop Nicholas Ridley who was burned at the stake in Oxford in 1555 for his religious beliefs. But the Ridleys were not all saints. At that time this was officially Border country, where the laws and mores of England did not apply. Cross-border forays were even encouraged by some kings to keep their opponents off-balance. The name of Ridley was often to the fore where there was trouble.

✳ The serrated ridge continues east from Turret 44B, with two more energy-sapping dips and ascents. (These can be avoided by using the Military Way, just to the south – but this does not enjoy the same views from the crags, and besides, it is a bit late now!) Continue over Muckleback Crag, north of Allolee with its protective belt of trees, then descend gradually along the rough ridge, or the Military Way, towards Cockmount Hill Farm.

Bypass the farm through the wood, and emerge through a gate onto the green Military Way. Follow this, or the line of the ditch, gently down to Great Chesters, where you can enter the Roman Fort of AESICA at its north-west corner.

● AESICA is probably a disappointment to most casual visitors. It has not been excavated for neat display like other forts, so there is little to see apart from the west wall remains, with a blocked-up gateway and corner turrets. The view is good!

AESICA: West Gate.

● Aesica was an infantry fort, commanding the gap in the crags caused by the Haltwhistle Burn. An intriguing feature for discerning map-readers is the camp water-supply: a 6-mile long aqueduct twists round the contours from its source 2½ miles away.

·245

AESICA ROMAN FORT

Greatchesters

0   ½   1km
© Crown Copyright.

Cawfields. car park, toilets, picnic area

stile   stile

VALLUM

FORT   Milecastle Inn

Tourist bus (summer).

paths to and from Haltwhistle

✱ From Great Chesters the path descends south-eastwards on the Military Way. Beyond Burnhead turn left to a stile. Across the bridge over the Caw Burn you reach the Cawfields picnic site and car-park.

Cawfields Quarry

105

Haltwhistle to Cawfields Milecastle and Great Chesters.

(5.5 km (3¼ miles) one-way, 9 km (5½ miles) circular.

❀ **Walk** up Haltwhistle's Main Street until a paved way goes steeply up to join the higher level. The path to Haltwhistle Burn leaves past a house and is easily mistaken for a garden path. It goes down beside a wall to the bank of the burn. Do not cross the bridge here but follow the delightful little valley upstream. Join a lane and continue beside the burn, and cross a bridge by the old colliery. Turn sharp left along the old railway line. Go round the bend & follow the path on upstream over a succession of footbridges. When you have left the trees and industrial relics behind, the path climbs up out of the valley to meet the Military Road (B6318). Follow it along to the Mile-Castle Inn (recrossing the burn en route). Turn left up the minor road. At the corner in the site of a Roman Fort,

a gate opens onto a field-path towards Cawfields Milecastle (visible to the right of the remnant peak left by Cawfields Quarry). You walk through another Roman camp and the impressive remains of the Vallum (the southern defensive perimeter of the Wall Zone). Climb up to the milecastle for a splendid view.

The gate through the Wall below the milecastle is the way west. The Pennine Way passes Cawfields Picnic Site to the lane. Cross the bridge, then follow the P.W. up the slope to Great Chesters (one of the great Wall forts - see following pages).

❀ Return can be made along the Great Chesters Farm access road, then by farm-roads past Lees Hall. These drop down by Broomshaw Hill Farm into the Haltwhistle Burn valley.

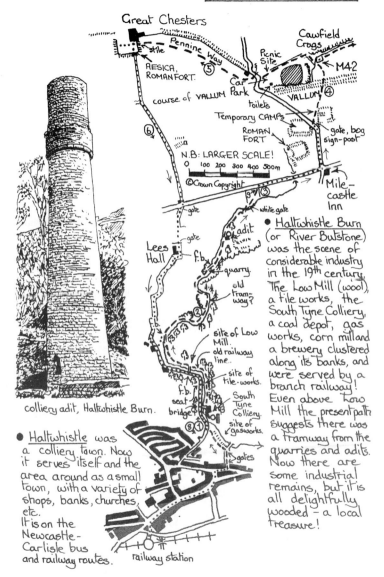

colliery adit, Haltwhistle Burn.

Great Chesters

Cawfield Crags

stile   Pennine Way

Picnic Site

M42

⑤

AESICA, ROMAN FORT.

course of VALLUM

Car Park

VALLUM ④

toilets

Temporary CAMPS

gate, bog sign-post

⑥

ROMAN FORT

N.B: LARGER SCALE!

0 100 200 300 400 500m

©Crown Copyright

Mile-castle Inn

gate

white gate

③

gate

adit

Lees Hall

f.b.

quarry

old tram-way?

f.b.

②

site of Low Mill.

old railway line

f.b.

seat

bridge

site of tile-works.

South Tyne Colliery.

site of gasworks.

⑧ ①

gates

railway station

• Haltwhistle Burn (or River Butstone) was the scene of considerable industry in the 19th century. The Low Mill (wool), a tile works, the South Tyne Colliery, a coal depot, gas works, corn mill and a brewery clustered along its banks, and were served by a branch railway! Even above Low Mill the present path suggests there was a tramway from the quarries and adits. Now there are some industrial remains, but it is all delightfully wooded – a local treasure!

• Haltwhistle was a colliery town. Now it serves itself and the area around as a small town, with a variety of shops, banks, churches, etc.
It is on the Newcastle-Carlisle bus and railway routes.

Cawfields

• Haltwhistle Burn makes a gap in the defensive line of crags that face north between the Rivers Irthing and North Tyne. So when the Romans drew back from Scotland in AD80 and established a defensive line across the land from Corbridge to Carlisle it made sense to build a fortlet beside the Stanegate and the burn. A study of the O.S. Map will reveal that the Romans established quite a few temporary camps in this area. (-a forerunner of the Otterburn Ranges perhaps?)

Later, after the death of the Emperor Trajan in 117 his successor Hadrian had problems on his frontiers. He set up a palisade and watch-towers across Germany, and the famous Wall between Newcastle and Carlisle to protect the strategic road — the Stanegate.

The milecastle is one of a series, a Roman mile apart.

- The <u>milecastle on Cawfields Crags</u> has been excavated and consolidated, to make its layout visible. The even spacing along the Wall has given it an excellent view but an awkward sloping site. Note how the stone courses follow the slope where it is not too steep. Gateways in north and south walls allowed quick access to either side of the wall for mounted troops. No trace remains of barrack huts within the milecastle.
- <u>Cawfields Quarry</u>, that ate a hill and 500m of Wall, is now a picnic site and car park (Northumberland National Park).

* The path from the National Park carpark, in the reclaimed Cawfields Quarry, passes the lake and climbs to a gate in Hadrian's Wall between the unmined remnant of the hill and Milecastle 42 (page 109). Follow the conserved section of Wall along the crest of Cawfields Crags and down into the dip of Thorny Doors. Climb steeply up again, following the Wall on past the excavated remains of suppressed turret 41A (above). Descend, muddily, to cross the lane in Caw Gap.

The Vallum, down to the right, is particularly obvious along this section of Wall.

Beyond Caw Gap the path climbs up the rocky slopes, following a tall dry-stone wall on the Wall foundations. It switch-backs along the north-facing rim of the Whinstone ridge (opposite page). Presently it rises up onto Winshields Crags, to the high-point of the Wall, 1230ft, 345 metres above sea-level at the Ordnance Survey triangulation pillar:

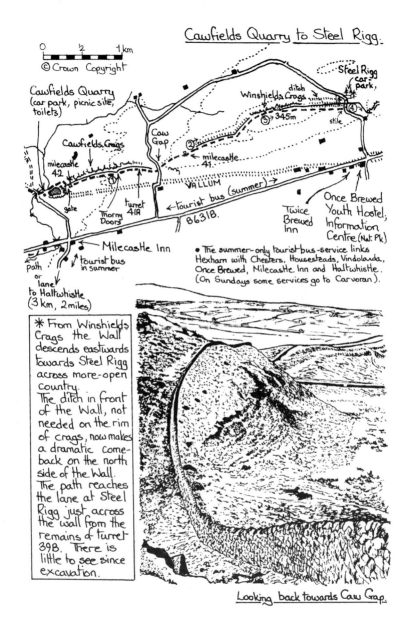

Cawfields Quarry to Steel Rigg.

0   ½   1 km

© Crown Copyright

Cawfields Quarry
(car park, picnic site, toilets)

Steel Rigg car park.

ditch

Winshields Crags

④

⑤ 345m

stile

Cawfields Crags

Cow Gap

milecastle 42

② ← milecastle 41

gate

③

Thorny Doors

turret 41A

VALLUM

← tourist bus (summer) →

B6318

Once Brewed Youth Hostel; Information Centre (Nat. Pk)

Twice Brewed Inn

— Milecastle Inn

↑ tourist bus in summer

path or lane ↓

to Haltwhistle (3 km, 2 miles)

• The summer-only tourist-bus-service links Hexham with Chesters, Housesteads, Vindolanda, Once Brewed, Milecastle Inn and Haltwhistle. (On Sundays some services go to Carvoran).

* From Winshields Crags the Wall descends eastwards towards Steel Rigg across more-open country.
The ditch in front of the Wall, not needed on the rim of crags, now makes a dramatic come-back on the north side of the Wall.
The path reaches the lane at Steel Rigg just across the wall from the remains of turret 39B. There is little to see since excavation.

Looking back towards Cow Gap.

<u>Steel Rigg to Housesteads</u>: 5.2 km (3¼ miles) of Roman Wall
(9 km (5½ miles) return). Energetic!

- <u>Steel Rigg</u> has a carpark and toilets (modern!). A turret, 39B, lurks in the wood where the Wall crosses the lane. Although excavated, little is visible now.
  The Wall goes east, wide enough to walk on. The National Trust is discouraging this practice – the Wall was built 1900 years ago to carry the occasional patrolling sentry, not the repeated compactions of thousands of tourists!
- <u>Peel Gap</u>, as its name implies, was long reputed to have had

a peel tower on the line of the Wall. But no trace was visible. In 1988 excavations revealed an extra turret on the Wall. It seems to have been added after the Wall was built. Perhaps this gap was a frequent trouble spot, requiring an extra presence to counter raiders or smugglers.

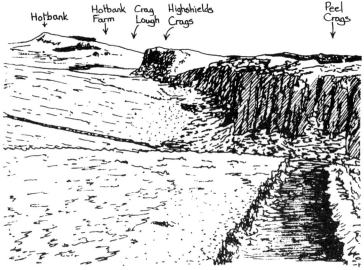

Hotbank Hotbank Crag Highshields   Peel
          Farm Lough Crags   Crags

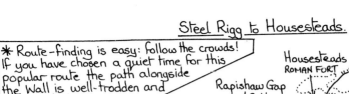

* Route-finding is easy: follow the crowds!
If you have chosen a quiet time for this
popular route the path alongside
the Wall is well-trodden and
sign-posted.

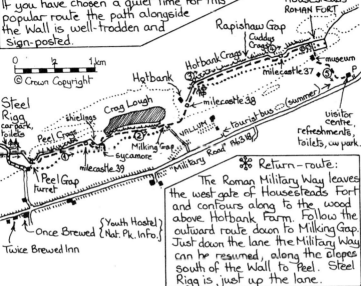

Housesteads
ROMAN FORT

Rapishaw Gap
Cuddy's Crags

Hotbank Crags

museum
milecastle 37

Hotbank

Crag Lough

milecastle 38

0   ½   1 km
© Crown Copyright

Steel Rigg
car park, toilets

shielings

Peel Crags

sycamore

milecastle 39

VALLUM

← tourist bus ⤳ (summer)

visitor centre, refreshments, toilets, car park.

Milking Gap

"Military Road" B6318

Peel Gap
turret

Once Brewed { Youth Hostel }
            { Nat. Pk. Info. }

Twice Brewed Inn

❄ Return-route:
    The Roman Military Way leaves
the west gate of Housesteads Fort
and contours along to the wood
above Hotbank Farm. Follow the
outward route down to Milking Gap.
Just down the lane the Military Way
can be resumed, along the slopes
south of the Wall to Peel. Steel
Rigg is just up the lane.

Peel Crags ↓

Barcombe

Peel Gap ↓

Steel Rigg to Housesteads : Milecastle 39

● <u>Peel Crags</u>: From Peel Gap the path climbs steeply up onto the top of the crags. Care is needed in wet or icy conditions. Along the top is a fine section of Wall, restored in 1969. It includes turret 39A, unusual in being built as a "narrow-gauge" turret — most turrets were built in the early, optimistic, full-width Wall era, even if the adjoining Wall was narrow.

● <u>Castle Nick</u>, the second dip, has <u>Milecastle 39</u>. This was excavated thoroughly in 1988. The gateways are built of ordinary-sized stones, where most milecastles have rather massive stonework. Perhaps its location posed more than usual transport problems! Within the fort are the remains of barrack rooms and stables.

● Just up to the east, overlooking Sycamore Gap, are further remains. These are not extra turrets, despite the excellent view, but shepherds' shielings. The Wall itself is not on the original foundations : these were uncovered in 1985, alongside.

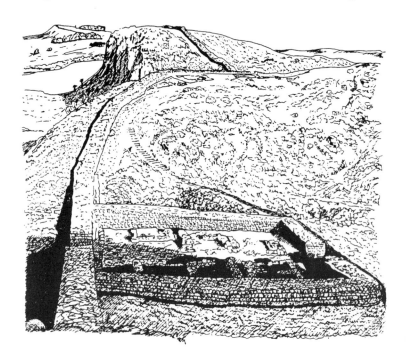

● <u>Sycamore Gap</u>: the renovated Wall drops steeply into the gap from both sides. The path crosses the Wall in the dip, passing the superb sycamore tree. As even trees are mortal, it is nice to see a successor being trained. Its protection is against sheep, which have changed this landscape from the scrubby woodland that the legions would have seen to this grassy desert.

- <u>Highshields Crags:</u> the tall climbs and good rock make this an excellent place to learn the art of rock-climbing – when suitably equipped of course! For ordinary travellers this is a delightful place, with a wood of Scots pine and sycamore and immense – and beautiful – views.
- <u>Crag Lough</u> lies in the shelter of the crags, dark and serene. Swans and ducks may be seen, and boats too.

Steel Rigg to Housesteads: Hotbank and Cuddy's Crags.

● <u>Hotbanks Farm</u> has a magnificent location, overlooking Crag Lough and Milking Gap. Just below it, on the line of the Wall, is Milecastle 38. This has been thoroughly robbed of facing stone, but its outline can still be traced in the rank grass.

● <u>Hadrian's Wall</u> resumes above the farm, and runs along the top of Hotbank Crags. Greenlee Lough is visible to the north. Turrets on this section have been suppressed – replaced by plain wall. This drops steeply into <u>Rapishaw Gap</u>, where the Pennine Way departs northwards towards Wark Forest and Bellingham. A barrier of rocks on the east side of the Gap can be avoided to the south.

● <u>Cuddy's Crags</u> continue to another steep-sided Gap. Steps lead up onto Housesteads Crags

● <u>Milecastle 37</u> is neatly excavated, and shows some massive gateway stonework. Just beyond is <u>House-steads Wood</u>:

Housesteads

● Housesteads Roman Fort is a pleasant surprise after the disappointments of the forts at Carvoran and Aesica. This fort has been excavated and displayed for the public by English Heritage (The National Trust owns the land). Detailed guides are available from the Museum (near the fort) or from the Visitors' Centre (at the carpark). There is a visitor's fee too!

Perhaps the first surprise is its size: nearly five acres (2 hectares). Then its location: hard up against the Wall on the Whin Sill crags. The views are magnificent. This was not a soft posting for its garrison (mainly a Belgium-originating battalion – the Tungrians). It is high on the crags in the wilds. Even water was scarce, as the rock under the fort itself was too hard for the Romans to dig a well. Drinking water had to be brought up from the Knag Burn.

Housesteads was an afterthought for the Wall, as defensive tactics changed. Instead of servicing the Wall from forts on the Stanegate (the trade road), the new idea was for forts actually on the Wall, linked together by a new Military Way. Turret 36B, already built, had to be demolished to build the fort.

The Military Way entered and left the fort by the East and the West gateway (below). The Military Way is a useful return route to Hotbank and Steel Rigg.

Because of the crags and the slope the fort was built with its long axis east-west, the Wall forming its long north Wall, (unlike Chesters which sits astride the Wall). Two more gates, in the north and south walls, controlled trade between the "wilds" and the "civilized" world, and allowed rapid military deployment when necessary.

● The standard of Roman engineering was better than any other in Britain for a thousand years to follow. You can see remnants here in the carefully engineered water flow and conservation system. Rain-water was collected in stone cisterns and channelled to where it was needed, such as the <u>latrines</u> (above). The waste was put to use on the system of cultivation terraces outside the walls.

In the centre of the fort was the <u>headquarter's building</u> (below), a building of style, despite the wild surroundings.

Housesteads

● The fort itself is clearly presented for visitors to inspect, with information boards sited at useful points. Visitors of all ages will find something here to interest them (Even if it is just the stones on the sub-floor of the impressive granaries!)

But visitors have not always been welcome. In the Middle Ages this was the lair of the Armstrongs, local outlaws. They built a bastle-tower against the south gateway of the fort, with a kiln through the wall in the old gatehouse. As England became too civilized for them, the clan sold up and emigrated to America.

The small town that grew up on the slopes outside the south gate in Roman times gave the present name: house-steads. Some has been excavated but little is displayed. Other Roman remains in the area — temples on Chapel Hill and near the Knag Burn, and the bath-house, are similarly not presently on display.

But the museum and the Visitors' Centre do have exhibits that show how the fort worked, what it probably looked like, and what life was like for the Wall garrison.
The Visitors' Centre (National Trust, free) also has a shop, a picnic site and simple refreshments on sale. Summer buses, too.

Housesteads

- Knag Burn gatehouse
- Military Way to Sewingshields.
- North Gate
- granary
- well
- Bath-house (not visible)
- Cuddy's Crags
- cistern
- latrines
- Roman Military Way
- South Gate and Armstrong Bastle
- West Gate
- H.Q.
- town
- terraces
- line of Roman road.
- museum
- farm
- line of VALLUM
- well
- temple (not visible)
- Chapel Hill
- Visitors' Centre and carpark.
- HOUSESTEADS: NOT TO SCALE
- Mithraeum (not visible)
- to Vindolanda
- summer bus service

Housesteads North Gateway.
(The cistern on the left was to catch rainwater, not to wash captured Britons!)

Housesteads to Vindolanda or Bardon Mill

3.6 km (2.4 miles) or 5.3 km (3.4 miles) of upland paths and quiet lanes.

✱ The Roman road from Housesteads to Vindolanda is followed by the farm-track, down past the museum to cross the Vallum in the hollow then up onto the undulating moor. to meet the B6318. O.S. Maps show the continuing bridleway starting some 120 metres to the east, but there is no gate nor even stile at that point. But there are both just along to the right. The path drops into a dip, then climbs to a gap in the broken ridge. Beyond the gap the path disappears. But keep on southwards, up over the next little ridge and pick up the boggy path down to East Grindledikes. Follow the farm access-track up to meet the Stanegate, and turn right. Follow the once-important Roman road along the flank of Barcombe. This shows scars of mining and quarrying. After 600 metres or so you reach a road junction, and a decision whether to head for Bardon Mill directly or visit Vindolanda:

✱ For Vindolanda turn right down the lane past Grindledikes lime-kiln. A gate allows you to turn back on a field-path through the fascinating remains of the old colliery railway. Note the bridge under the road junction up above. The path follows the line of a siding to a quarry on Barcombe, to a stile onto the road. Follow the road below Barcombe and turn down to Chesterholm and Vindolanda. (You recross the old railway just after the small carpark).

✱ For Bardon Mill turn left over a wall-stile and up over the ridge. Descend the boggy southern flank to pick up the lane to West End Town. There turn right into the farm-yard, then left down the fields to the lane above Bardon Mill. Go left and down, under the A69 to the old main road, and right into the village.

122

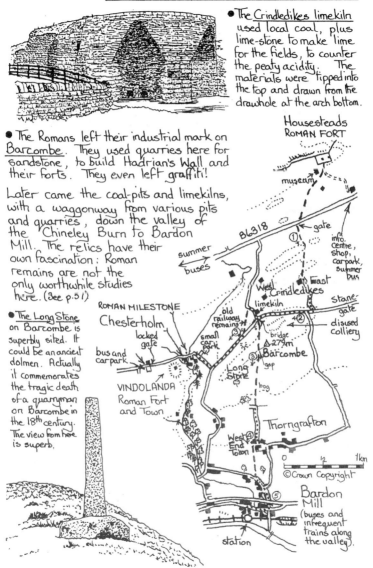

- The <u>Crindledikes limekiln</u> used local coal, plus lime-stone to make lime for the fields, to counter the peaty acidity. The materials were tipped into the top and drawn from the drawhole at the arch bottom.

- The Romans left their industrial mark on <u>Barcombe</u>. They used quarries here for sandstone, to build Hadrian's Wall and their forts. They even left graffiti!

Later came the coal-pits and limekilns, with a waggonway from various pits and quarries, down the valley of the Chineley Burn to Bardon Mill. The relics have their own fascination: Roman remains are not the only worthwhile studies here. (See p.51)

- The <u>Long Stone</u> on Barcombe is superbly sited. It could be an ancient dolmen. Actually it commemorates the tragic death of a quarryman on Barcombe in the 18th century. The view from here is superb.

Housesteads
ROMAN FORT

museum

B6318

gate

info. centre, shop, carpark, summer bus

summer buses

West Crindledikes limekiln

East Crindledikes

stane gate

disused colliery

ROMAN MILESTONE

Chesterholm

locked gate

bus and carpark

old railway remains

small car park

bridge

△279m

Barcombe

gap

bog

Long Stone

VINDOLANDA
Roman Fort and Town

Thorngrafton

West End Town

0   ½   1km

©Crown Copyright

Bardon Mill
(buses and infrequent trains along the valley).

station

123

● Vindolanda is one of the most fascinating Roman sites in Britain — not particularly for its Roman fort remains, but for the excavated town alongside, and the extraordinary treasures that have been unearthed. Unlike previous generations of finds these have not been whisked away to museums in Newcastle, Durham or London, but are presented here, in the museum of Chesterholm.

Chesterholm was built in 1831 for the Rev. Anthony Hedley, who established a reputation for detailed recording of layouts of Roman forts. Now, still in an idyllic setting beside the burns, with trees and gardens surrounding it, it houses the Vindolanda Trust's museum, coffee-shop and bookshop.

The museum is superbly laid out, with informative displays that show the finds and how they were used, with replicas to show how they would have looked when new. Here are letters and leatherwork, sandals and Samian ware, arms and ornaments. It is fascinating. Spend some time here!

Barcombe, from Vindolanda

● The visible Roman fort is in the care of English Heritage. It is the newest (only 16 centuries old) of a series of forts on this site. The first, built before the Wall to control the Stanegate, lies some six metres below the surface. This is well appreciated by viewing the fort mound from the Stanegate (the lane running past on the north side). Newer forts were built as defensive strategies changed. The site was even abandoned for a while when Housesteads became the local operations-centre. Later forts were built facing different ways on more or less the same site. On view in the fort are the well-designed 4th century headquarters building in the centre, and gateways to north and west (below).

Vindolanda: the town.

● The really unusual feature of Vindolanda is that it is the town outside the fort that is receiving nearly all the attention. In the 1st to 4th centuries A.D. there was a succession of dwellings, making a multi-layered cake for the archaeologists to explore. This can be appreciated best if any deep work is taking place when you visit. The sealing-over of earlier remains, plus the generally damp condition of the soil, has preserved many items that normally would have rotted away, notably wooden writing-tablets (with writing!), leather sandals, food and bedding debris and fragments of cloth.

Many surface buildings have been opened up and consolidated for display. There is an inn, and married quarters for the later farmer-soldiers. There are wells, cisterns and aqueducts. The impressive bath-house may be looked at — but not touched: its condition, with plaster still adhering to the stonework in places, is too fragile to withstand the erosive power of contact with thousands of visitors.

Vindolanda is very much an active centre of excavation. You can learn much by watching the work. Vigilant visitors may even make finds themselves on the field. (If you do, report it!) But do respect the dig-sites and the fenced-off areas, for your own safety and that of the workers!

Vindolanda : the Replicas.

• South of the excavations stands a feature that excites visitors and infuriates some members of the archaeological Establishment: the Replica Wall. This was built in 1972-4 by staff and pupils of Heathfield Senior High School in Gateshead. It comprises a length of Turf Wall (as used in Cumberland) with a timber milecastle gateway, and a length of stone wall with stone turret. Detail above existing Wall-level is conjectural, but the process of building the Replicas and observation of the way that they have weathered have been illuminating. Notice how much the Turf Wall has shrunk, so that steps are necessary to reach the gateway doors.

Replica gateway and Turf Wall.

Replica turret and stone wall

127

Housesteads to Sewingshields.   2.8km, (1¾ miles) of Roman Wall.

✱ From Housesteads you can follow either side of the Wall
north-eastwards down the bank to the Knag Burn. Leave
the fort by the west gate and cross the Wall at the corner,
or follow the Military Way out of the east gate .....

● At the burn you will find a rarity: a gate through the Wall
that is not at a fort or milecastle. It was added long after
the Wall was built, in the 4ᵗʰ century, allowing civilian traffic
to bypass the fort (and the climb to its north gate!) A pair of
gate-houses allowed for rigorous customs control on this
boundary of the Roman Empire.

✱ Beyond the gateway climb the bank on the east side of
the Wall. At the stile into the wood look back for the view
of Housesteads. Beyond the wood follow the line of the
wall (not excavated) to the north-east, over King's Hill
towards Sewingshields Crags, that rise dramatically ahead.
This is good walking.

Housesteads to Sewingshields.

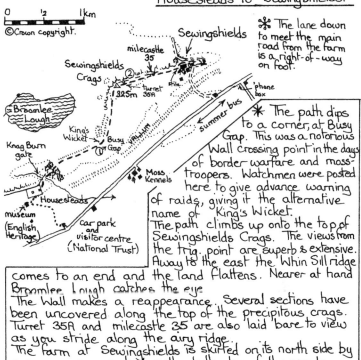

❋ The lane down to meet the main road from the farm is a right-of-way on foot.

❋ The path dips to a corner, at Busy Gap. This was a notorious Wall crossing point in the days of border warfare and moss-troopers. Watchmen were posted here to give advance warning of raids, giving it the alternative name of King's Wicket.

The path climbs up onto the top of Sewingshields Crags. The views from the trig. point are superb & extensive. Away to the east the Whin Sill ridge comes to an end and the land flattens. Nearer at hand Broomlee Lough catches the eye.

The Wall makes a reappearance. Several sections have been uncovered along the top of the precipitous crags. Turret 35A and milecastle 35 are also laid bare to view as you stride along the airy ridge.

The farm at Sewingshields is skirted on its north side by a narrow waymarked path at the top of the woods.

<u>Sewingshields to Brocolitia</u> 5.3 km (3.4 miles), initially on a rough track, but nearly 4km on roads (at the time of writing)

✻ East of Sewingshields the path descends to cross the track from Stell Green just south of the cottage.
Continue eastwards on the boggy track that follows the Military Way, south of the line of the Wall.
Turret 34A stands proud of the turf upon the left. Further on, as the land flattens the Ditch reappears. Milecastle 34 is marked by a walled copse.
Coesike Turret, 33B, is the last on this section of Wall before the road is met.
. . . . .

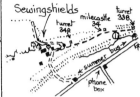

• <u>Grindon Turret, 34A</u>. This turret, like 35A up on the crags, and 33B at Coesike, was suppressed by the Romans, who reduced it to plain wall (presumably when the accountants required a "down-sizing" of the garrison). The narrow wall inside the turret was filled out to standard Wall width. At Coesike this infill has subsided, due to lack of proper foundations.

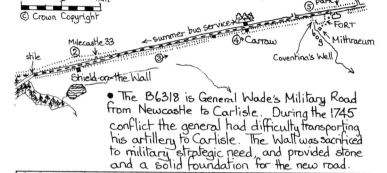

© Crown Copyright

The B6318 is General Wade's Military Road from Newcastle to Carlisle. During the 1745 conflict the general had difficulty transporting his artillery to Carlisle. The Wall was sacrificed to military strategic need, and provided stone and a solid foundation for the new road.

✳ Perhaps it will not be long before a right-of-way on foot is established parallel to the road, but in the meantime there is no alternative to walking along the road. It is not without interest: the Ditch keeps it company on the north side, and the Vallum and its parapets are clearly seen to the south.

● <u>Brocolitia and the Mithraeum.</u> The Roman fort—an after-thought on the Wall—is unexcavated at present. Down by the south-west corner, in a waterlogged hollow, are the fascinating remains of a temple to Mithras, an Irano-Indian sun god adopted by many in the Roman Army. The boggy conditions caused by nearby Coventina's Well kept its buried timbers free from rot. Concrete casts of the original altars and wooden pillars show the site as excavated. The original altars are in a reconstructed temple in Newcastle.

131

Brocolitia to Chesters   5.5km (3½ miles) – all on the road.

> ✳ Return to the road, past the car-park. Head east. The line of the Vallum, between its ramparts, is clear on the south side of the road, as is the Roman Military Way. But there is no public path. Even the road, which is busy in summer, has no footway. So keep one eye on the scenery, and one on the traffic! A bridleway heading south offers an opportunity to sample the cross-section of the Vallum works. Continue along the road to Limestone Corner.

The 'Hadrian's Wall' bus service runs along the road in summer.

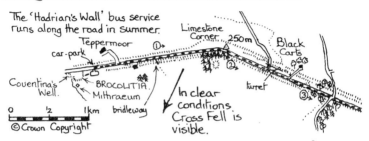

● Limestone Corner. The line of the Ditch veers away from the road at the corner, gleaning the maximum tactical advantage from the terrain. The Ditch is unfinished here: huge blocks of hard limestone litter its floor and sides. The Vallum, in contrast, is fully finished, perhaps showing its greater importance. At the corner you cross a watershed. The broad valley ahead belongs to the North Tyne. The South Tyne has curved away to the south round Warden Hill.

Limestone Corner.

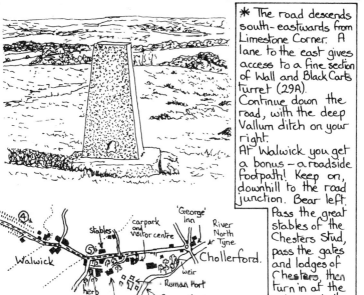

* The road descends south-eastwards from Limestone Corner. A lane to the east gives access to a fine section of Wall and Black Carts turret (29A). Continue down the road, with the deep Vallum ditch on your right.

At Walwick you get a bonus — a roadside footpath! Keep on, downhill to the road junction. Bear left. Pass the great stables of the Chesters Stud, pass the gates and lodges of Chesters, then turn in at the entrance to the fort and museum.

The Ditch and Wall at Black Carts.

Chesters Roman Fort

- The Roman ruins at Chesters — the cavalry fort, town and bath-house — were levelled at the end of the 18th century when the new owner, Nathaniel Clayton, wanted an uninterrupted park between his home and the river. So each of the sites visible sits in a little hollow, with railings round to keep the animals out (or the visitors in). Most of this excavation was led by John Clayton in the mid 19th century, and much still remains to be uncovered of the fort and of the town to the south. Now it is in the care of English Heritage (who publish a detailed guide and map).

North Gateway.

- There are six gateways — at north and south ends, and two on east and west sides. This was a cavalry fort, supporting the Roman Wall (which originally ran through the centre of the site). Quick exits were an essential feature of the design, although the double gateways were later reduced to single width as the forts developed a passive defensive role.
- A large headquarters building is in the middle of the fort, and one of the barracks has been excavated in the NE corner.

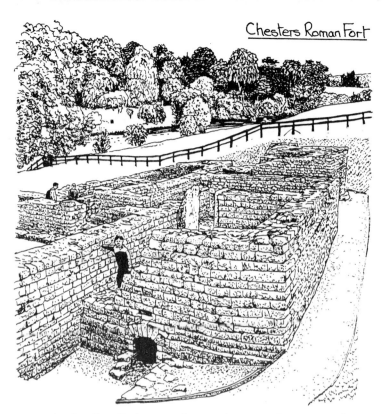

● Outside the fort, on the bank down towards the North Tyne, is the Bath-house, perhaps the most interesting building for casual visitors. Here, with a little imagination — to reclothe the ashlar walls with plaster and the floors with mosaics — you can conjure up the life-style of the garrison. Here was the social centre, the club-house on the riverbank. It offered a level of provision that the English have only re-adopted in the 20th century — hot baths, saunas, cold dips, warm rooms. Yes, this is impressive!

● The museum is a fascinating old-fashioned collection of artifacts large and small. Unfortunately the space is too limited for the modern educational displays that would put these wonderful things into context. We can but hope!

Chollerford

is the lowest bridging point on the North Tyne.
- The Romans built a bridge to carry first the Wall, then their Military Way as well, a kilometre downstream from the present bridge. The remains are worth a visit.

> ✳ To visit the Roman Bridge go to the south end of the bridge at Chollerford. A sign-posted gate allows you down onto a long, narrow, wired-in footpath that leads you to the east abutment. As you walk along the narrow path, alongside the broad trackbed of the erstwhile Border Counties Railway, ponder the ways of the bureacratic mind! Return the same way.

- On the east bank of the North Tyne, under the trees, you can see the massive <u>east abutment</u> (right). Its huge stone blocks, cunningly tied together with lead-bound iron, are now some way back from the wandering river. Other piers may be visible in the river-bed. Across the river are the baths of Chesters. The bridge was <u>big</u>, 6 metres (20') in width, carrying the Wall plus Military Way on four arches 58m (190') across the river. It replaced an earlier bridge that carried just the Wall.

- The 'modern' bridge dates from 1775, replacing a medieval bridge swept away by the great flood of 1771. Again it was serving a Military purpose: the Hanoverian government had been caught out by James Stuart's attack down the west side of the Pennines in 1715. After the '45 they were moved to action: a Military Road for all weathers was built from Newcastle to Carlisle, using many miles of Roman Wall for foundations and materials.

- Chollerford can be reached by the service buses from Hexham to Bellingham, or on the summer-only Hadrians Wall Coach service that links Hexham, Chollerford, Housesteads, Steel Rigg, Vindolanda, Greenhead and Haltwhistle.

- The 'George' is located conveniently next to the bridge.

Chesters to Warden 7.0 km (4½ miles) of lanes and hillpaths.

* The Roman fort is in the midst of the private grounds of Chesters, so you will have to return to the road. Turn west, (left) up the hill, and walk up past the gate lodges and the majestic stables of Chesters to the junction with the Haydon Bridge road. Turn left down it.

Almost at once another distraction offers itself: Hexham Herbs, in the walled garden of Chesters, is a delight.

Continue down the tree-lined road, and follow it round to the right outside the gates of Walwick Grange. (The quiet lane diverging to the left goes directly to Warden.) Go up the road onto the ridge. A signposted gate shows the way into the fields, heading down then across to the shoulder of Warden Hill. A large solitary ash stands beside the path as it starts to wind up over the lee. Suddenly the view changes: ahead is the broad valley of the South Tyne as it comes down from Haydon Bridge to Fourstones, before curving round the foot of the hill.

Keep on the path round the hillside until you meet a track coming up from Fourstones. Do not go through the gate, but turn up beside the wall towards a cottage tucked up under the woods. Pass right, through a pair of gates, onto a path heading south along the lower edge of the wood.

The path divides. Turn uphill through the pines and emerge onto the hilltop field. (The hill is crowned with an ancient fort and a trig. point : a path goes up beside the wall). But our way heads down diagonally for the south-east corner, where beyond a gate you meet a track. This goes down the ridge, past a transmitter for portable telephones, towards High Warden.

Enjoy the wide views. The track slides off the ridge by a wood, down to High Warden. Turn left, passing the walled garden, then at a junction among the buildings go half-left onto a steeply descending track. Beyond the cattle grid turn off down the slope to meet the lane to Warden at a gate below. Follow the delightful lane (left) down to Warden.

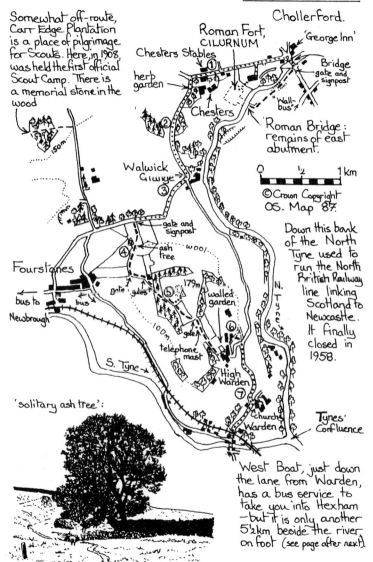

Chollerford.

Roman Fort, CILURNUM

'George Inn'

Chesters Stables

Bridge gate and signpost

herb garden

"Wall-bus"

Chesters

Roman Bridge: remains of east abutment.

Somewhat off-route, Carr Edge Plantation is a place of pilgrimage for Scouts. Here, in 1908, was held the first official Scout Camp. There is a memorial stone in the wood

150m

Walwick Grange

3

0   ½   1 km

© Crown Copyright
OS. Map 87.

Down this bank of the North Tyne used to run the North British Railway line linking Scotland to Newcastle. It finally closed in 1958.

gate and signpost

ash tree

wool

Fourstones

bus to Newbrough

bus

gate gates

179m

5

walled garden

6

N. Tyne

100m

gate

telephone mast

S. Tyne

High Warden

7

Church
Warden

Tynes' Confluence

'solitary ash tree':

West Boat, just down the lane from Warden, has a bus service to take you into Hexham —but it is only another 5½km beside the river on foot (see page after next).

139

Warden to Hexham 5.5 km (3½ miles) of mainly riverside paths.

● Warden is a charming place, set here at the junction of two rivers. Its Saxon church is a delight. Details and pictures are on pages 76 and 77.

Presumably this was a place where travellers could be stranded in bad weather, before the modern bridges were built. If the rivers were too deep to ford and too fast for the ferry-boat one had to wait....

Nowadays you can catch a bus from the Boatside Inn to take you into Hexham, or you can cross the bridge and walk.

If you are not too tired to care, you will notice that this section has been walked before, at the end of Ch. Two.

If you do decide to wait for a bus, or if you need refreshment before continuing, you may be fortunate enough to find the inn open:

✳ From Warden walk down the lane to West Boat. Cross the bridge and turn left, along the lane. Just beyond the first houses look for the start of the riverside path. It starts beside a house drive and disappears into the bushes behind house gardens. Follow the riverside path downstream, under the railway and past the confluence of the two Tynes. Continue under the A69 road-bridge .....

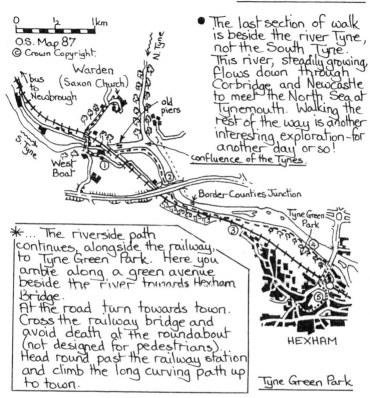

O.S. Map 87
© Crown Copyright.

Warden
(Saxon Church)

bus to
Newbrough

old piers

S. Tyne

West Boat

N. Tyne

confluence of the Tynes.

Border Counties Junction

Tyne Green Park

• The last section of walk is beside the river Tyne, not the South Tyne. This river, steadily growing, flows down through Corbridge, and Newcastle to meet the North Sea at Tynemouth. Walking the rest of the way is another interesting exploration - for another day or so!

HEXHAM

✱... The riverside path continues, alongside the railway, to Tyne Green Park. Here you amble along a green avenue beside the river towards Hexham Bridge.
At the road turn towards town. Cross the railway bridge and avoid death at the roundabout (not designed for pedestrians). Head round past the railway station and climb the long curving path up to town.

Tyne Green Park

141

Chapter Four: Hexham

is a town of contrasts. Here are ancient fortified buildings and an abbey, dominating the high centre of town. But here too are the sprawls of modern shopping centres and carparks. Here is the mediaeval market town – updated – and also factories, belching forth clouds of steam and smoke that can be seen for miles. Here are the narrow streets of town and the broad parks of Tyne Green. Hexham, then, is a live town, rooted in its past and not forgetting it, but also firmly in the present and looking to the future. Hexham has dominated the mid-Tyne valleys for a thousand years, and intends to keep it that way!

Hexham Moot Hall

Hexham Gaol
or
Manor Office.

✳ From Hexham Bridge follow the road to the railway station, then follow the curving footpath that climbs up towards the high part of town, with the gaol, the Moot Hall, the market place and the Abbey.

• The Gaol was built in 1330, using Roman stonework, probably from Corbridge. It was built on the orders of the archbishop of York, who controlled Hexhamshire at that time. He used it to keep his tenants under firm control, as well as for occasional captives from the wild Border lands. From the late sixteenth century it was used as the archbishops Manor Office. Now it is a tourist information office, and houses an interesting little museum of Border life and history, the Middle March museum.

• The <u>Moot Hall</u>, the impressive gateway to the Abbey market-place, housed the archbishop's bailiff, and was his courtroom for Hexhamshire. It was in use as a court-house until 1838.

* Pass through the arch of the Moot Hall

• Hexham has been an important centre for the Tyne valley since Saxon times. The establishment of a great church in the late seventh century, and of the Priory in 1113 provided spurs for economic development. Hexham had reasonable fords for access to the North Tyne and the bounty of the south-facing slopes, and good ridge routes south onto the high Pennine roads. A chartered <u>market</u> and fairs were granted by Henry <u>III</u> in 1239.

The market place had a market cross until it was removed to Haydon Bridge in 1766. <u>The Temperley Memorial Fountain</u> was erected in 1901 to replace an earlier pant.

144

The Shambles, on the south side of the Market Square is a covered market, its roof supported on elegant stone columns on the north side, and square wooden ones to the south.

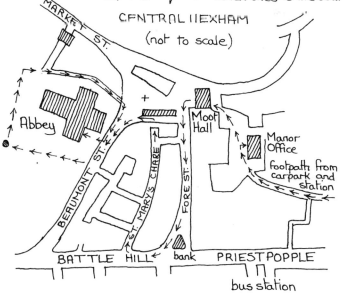

CENTRAL HEXHAM
(not to scale)

MARKET ST.

Abbey

BEAUMONT ST.

Moot Hall

Manor Office

footpath from carpark and station

ST. MARYS CHARE

FORE ST.

BATTLE HILL

bank

PRIEST POPPLE

bus station

Hexham: the town.

● Hexham is a busy country market town. South of the market square is an area of shops and banks, that cluster thickly around Fore Street, Priestpopple, Battle Hill and St. Mary's Chare. Here you will find all kinds of shops, from greengrocers to department stores, from bakers to antique dealers, and fossils. There is a variety of banks, and a post office. Pubs and inns too!

● In Priestpopple is the busy bus-station, whence buses leave for Newcastle and Carlisle, and all points along the Tyne: Alston, Haltwhistle, Bardon Mill, Haydon Bridge, Newbrough, West Boat, Chollerford..... In the summer a bus operates from here to points along Hadrian's Wall.

The Royal Hotel, Priestpopple

146

* A taster of the charms of Hexham's commercial area can be had by going south from the market square along Fore Street.

• At the south end of Fore Street you will find the fascinating Midland Bank building, occupying a triangular site. Where else will you find a bank being wrapped by cherubs?

* Turn right, very briefly up Battle Hill, then right into St Mary's Chare.

• St. Mary's Chare provides a quiet contrast to the bustle of Fore Street. Known locally as Back Street, it is much more interesting to explore.

• At the north end of St. Mary's Chare you come to the archway of Old Church.
This is one of the remnants of the old parish church of St. Mary, that used to stand along the south side of the market square.
After the Dissolution the priory church took over as parish church and St Mary's was absorbed into the town: pillars and arches can be found incorporated into the later buildings.

Hexham Abbey: a brief history

• St Wilfrid established the Christian church in Hexham, following a grant of land — the Regality of Hexhamshire — by the Queen of Northumbria, Etheldreda. The abbey that he built from 674 AD onwards was one of the wonders of civilised Europe. Acca, Wilfrid's successor, kept up the good work. But in 875 AD the magnificence and importance of the church of St. Andrew in Hexham did not stop Halfdene the Dane from burning it to the ground. All that remains of that early building is the crypt, the bishop's stool, Acca's Cross and various Saxon stones now built into the nave.

After an unsettled time of raids and wars, with the land pillaged by the Danes and then laid waste by the Normans from England, Hexham was resettled by the Archbishop of York in 1113, as an Augustinian priory. The good lands of Hexhamshire ensured that the priory flourished for many years.

But the Scots paid a visit in 1296, firing and gutting the priory. They enjoyed it so much that they came back the following year. (Only later did they change to holidays in Whitley Bay!). The canons could no longer prove title to their lands, all the deeds having been burnt, and had to reestablish their title at a special court set up by Edward I of England.

Repeated Scottish excursions kept the priory poor for fifty years or so, but the following peace allowed a return to prosperity, which encouraged lapses in monastic austerity.

The Dissolution of the minor religious houses in 1536 was resisted in Hexhamshire: the King's Commissioners were confronted by a local 'army' and were forced to retreat until the Duke of Norfolk arrived to suppress this "Pilgrimage of Grace". The priory church survived because it became the parish church, taking over from St. Mary's.

In 1583 the Regality of Hexhamshire formally became part of Northumberland, ending the distinction whereby the Bishop of York held full regal powers within the shire.

The priory church was to suffer further changes. It had lost its monastic buildings following the Dissolution. In Victorian eyes it should stand separate from the buildings of the market place. The shops were removed. The east front of the church was remodelled — then fell off! A replacement east front was built on, modelled on Whitby Abbey, but this design required a steeply pitched roof that does not match the shallow pitch of the 15th century roofs used in the rest of the church. It shows!

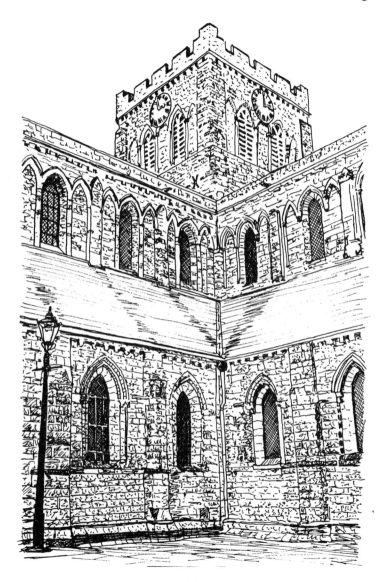

Hexham Abbey

* Before entering the Abbey it is worthwhile to make a turn around the outside (except in rain or fog, of course). Cross the market square and head south-west down Beaumont Street to the park entrance. Head west to the bandstand, then north, round the west end of the Abbey, to meet a little lane. Go east, through the smaller archway and along the Flag walk past the north transept. Back at the Market Place go past the 'new' east front to the Abbey entrance.

• Things to notice on the circuit:

• the east end of the chancel is newer than the rest. The 13th century east front was replaced in Victorian times — and then the Victorian front fell off! The new roof is steeper than the old, giving a distinct "hen-coop" on top of the east end.

• the chancel and south transept have simple lancet windows in the aisles, with corresponding lancets above in the clerestory, framed by blank arcades.

• nearly all the buildings of the monastery, to the south and west of the church, have gone. Fragments remain.

• the Abbey grounds, now a beautiful park, were a gift to the town. The bandstand is early 20th century.

• St. Wilfrid's Gate is the large gateway between the Abbey and Market Street. It was the original Abbey gatehouse. It gives some idea of the scale and strength of the walls that used to ring the Abbey for defence.

• The Nave (the western part of the church) is newer than the rest of the church. The mediaeval abbey had no need of a nave — the public part of the church — as the town had St. Mary's just across the square. A nave was not built with the rest after the Scots raids. After the Dissolution the townspeople could use the transepts. But in 1725 a buttress had to be added to the west side of the tower, as the tower was starting to subside due to the lack of a nave. A single bay — still apparent, was built in 1870. A complete nave, to the Augustinian pattern with a north aisle but no south aisle, was built in 1907-9 in a plain style that complements the older building without pretending to be mediaeval.

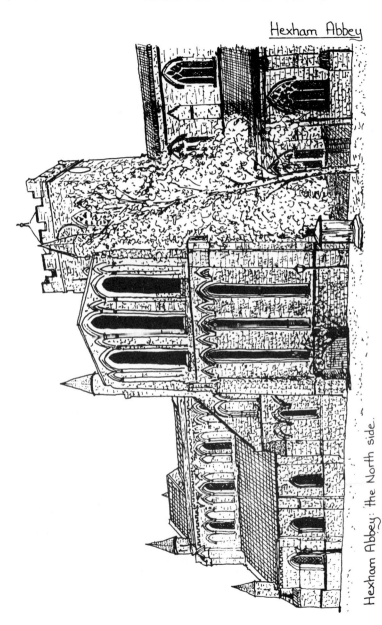

Hexham Abbey

Hexham Abbey: the North side.

Hexham Abbey

The South Transept and the Night Stairs.

> ✱ Enter the Abbey from the Market Place. The way in is through the Slype — a porch formed, unusually, in the last bay of the South Transept.

● In the South Transept the most striking feature is the Night Stairs. Such stairs, from the canons' dormitory usually came down into the cloister, ie on the outside of the wall, whereas this one unusually descends inside. Nowadays it is the Song School behind the gallery door, and the choir that descends the stairs.

● The re-assembled fragments of Acca's Cross stand on the east side of the transept. This was probably the headstone cross that marked the Saxon grave of Acca, a bishop.

● Almost opposite, in the old doorway to the cloister, stands an impressive stone nearly 3 metres high: the memorial stone to Flavinus, a Roman standard bearer. Flavinus, in full uniform with plumed helmet, carries a standard of the sun god, and rides over a Briton who is killing his horse.

● The Nave, on the west side, is in a Decorated style. Late Victorian, it stands where the mediaeval nave should have stood. The first bay, with weathered stones, was built in 1870 to support the tower, and the rest later, in 1905-8. The north aisle and west wall contain Saxon stones found during the building.

● The crypt is the oldest part of the church. It is sometimes open, and may be entered from the Nave.

● The North Transept is fascinating. Here is a place to sit in quiet and contemplate. The window is simple but elegant. The arches are complex and thought-provoking. The faith that produced all this 700 years ago is inspiring.

Hexham Abbey

- The chancel is a sumptuous contrast to the elegant simplicity of the Nave and transepts. Here the designers and architects have let themselves go in their celebration of the majesty and mystery of God, and the power of certain of His people. This part of the church feels dark and mediæval — or is it just that my visits have been at the end of the day? It starts with the Choir Screen, separating the men of the church from the hoi-polloi, with carving and painting and dark varnish. Here are panels of dark wood, choir stalls and 15th century carved misericords. Small chantries stand on either side like ornate cages, surrounded by more carvings and paintings. The altar stands raised up, before a tremendous Altar Screen and ornate cross. Saints peer down from the late Victorian east window.

But the lasting impression is made by the simplest artefact — the bishop's stool. This throne, possibly Wilfred's from the 7th century, has been moved from the side of the chancel to a central position in the choir. Carved from a single block of stone, its seat is highly polished from the thousands who have sat in it over the centuries. It is the Frith stool, or Peace seat — the traditional place of sanctuary. It is a good place to end our walk from the wilds of Cross Fell! Like sanctuary seekers, we can spend a short while in peace here, before heading downriver again towards the sea.

Bibliography

The following books have been useful or interesting during the research for this volume, and may be so to you too:

The King's England : Northumberland, (N'land Ed^n C'ttee), 1952.
The King's England: the Lake Counties, A. Mee, (Hodder + Stoughton)1937.
Tynedale. Frank Graham, (Frank Graham) 1978
Portrait of Northumberland, Nancy Ridley (Robert Hale), 1965
The Buildings of England : Northumberland, N. Pevsner (Penguin) 1957.
Northumberland Villages. Godfrey Watson (Robert Hale) 1976
Portrait of the Pennines, Roger Redfern (Robert Hale) 1969
Highways and Byways in Northumbria, P.A. Graham (Macmillan) 1921
Northumbria, Edward Grierson (Collins) 1976
Northumbrian Heritage, Nancy Ridley (Robert Hale) 1968
Pennine Way Companion, A. Wainwright, (Westmoreland Gazette) 1968.
A Guide to the Pennine Way, C.J. Wright (Constable) 1967
Pennine Way North, Tony Hopkins (Aurum/O.S./Countryside) 1989.
Northumberland National Park, Tony Hopkins, (Webb + Bower) 1987
Northumberland National Park Guide, J. Philipson (HMSO), 1969
Walks for Motorists, Northumberland, N.Area Ramblers (F. Warne) 1981.
The Alternative Pennine Way, D Brook & P Hinchliffe (Cicerone) 1992
Walking in the North Pennines, Paddy Dillon (Cicerone) 1991.
Hadrian's Wall, Dudley Green (John Donald) 1992
Hadrian's Wall, Stephen Johnson, (Batsford / English Heritage) 1989
The Reiver's Way, H.O. Wade (Frank Graham) 1977.
Ramblers through Northumberland, N.Area Ramblers Assoc^n (F.Graham)1977
Ramblers' Tynedale, N. Area Ramblers Assoc^n (Harold Hill) 1968
Vindolanda : Roman Fort and Civilian Settlement, Robin Birley (F.G.) 1973
Discoveries at Vindolanda, Robin Birley (F.Graham) 1973.
Hadrian's Wall : Central Sector, Robin Birley (Frank Graham) 1972
Chesters Roman Fort, Eric Birley, (HMSO) 1960
Housesteads Roman Fort, Eric Birley (HMSO) 1952
Vindolanda in Colour, Robin Birley (Frank Graham) 1974
A Walk around Historic Hexham, Hexham Civic Society, 1985.
Come Walking in Alston Moor (E. Cumbria Countryside Project).
Mediaeval Castles, Towers, etc. T.H. Rowland, 1987.
Rural Branch Lines of Northumberland, C.R. Warn (F.Graham) 1975.
Border Country Branch Lines, Neil Caplan, (Ian Allan) 1981
North Eastern Branch Lines since 1925, K. Hoole, (Ian Allan) 1978
LNER Branch Lines, C.J. Gammell (Oxford) 1993
Walks in the Hadrian's Wall area, N'land Cty Council, 1982
A Guide to Hexham Abbey, Hexham Abbey, (undated).

Index

The index is in three sections : geographical
                                    Topical
                                    Hadrian's Wall .

Geographical :

Geographical (continued):

Topical:

Index.

Hadrian's Wall:

A personal page.

If you allow yourself to write in books, you may wish to use this page for notes – whether it is a record of walks; names of people you meet; comments on the beer in the pubs......

● The Book House,
half-way up Castle Street
in Warkworth is the home
of Sandhill Press. Here
also is a homely bookshop.
Drop in and buy something,
preferably another of
the author's books!

Other titles from Sandhill
Press are listed opposite.

● The Author.

Odd as it may seem, Ian Smith is not a native of these
parts. Although he has been in love with Northumberland
—and one of its girls — for over twenty years, he actually
lives in Thornaby, on the Tees. His origins are even
further afield, not even in the North: he hales from
Bromley in Kent! Having destroyed some people's illusions,
he hastily adds that he much prefers the North, and
Northumberland in particular!
Ian is a physics teacher, daily in touch with a high
technology world of equipment and computing. The
walking, photography, drawing and hand-writing is
a nice contrast.